Before You Write Yo

Before You Write Your Novel sets out the techniques and approaches that lay the perfect foundation for writing your first novel. This concise and readable guide addresses the major stumbling blocks of fiction-writing: the importance of planning and structure. This book covers the essential components of novel-writing including narrative, story, plot, pace, chronology, character arc and engagement techniques, as well as research, story-building, plotting and editing. Using an open and honest approach, feeding from his own experience as a published novelist and creative-writing teacher, James McCreet offers a guide to the structural mechanisms of the novel, helping you plan a first draft through to a finished novel.

James McCreet has worked as a teacher, a bookseller, an editor, a copywriter, and a journalist. He taught the MA Novel course at Sheffield Hallam University, UK.

Before You Write Your Novel

Essential skills for the first-time novelist

James McCreet

LONDON AND NEW YORK

First published 2016
by Routledge
2 Park Square, Milton Park, Abingdon, Oxon OX14 4RN

and by Routledge
711 Third Avenue, New York, NY 10017

Routledge is an imprint of the Taylor & Francis Group, an informa business

British Library Cataloguing-in-Publication Data
A catalogue record for this book is available from the British Library

Library of Congress Cataloging-in-Publication Data
A catalog record for this book has been requested

ISBN: 978-1-138-18672-9 (hbk)
ISBN: 978-1-138-18673-6 (pbk)
ISBN: 978-1-315-64364-9 (ebk)

Typeset in Sabon LT Std
by Swales & Willis Ltd, Exeter, Devon, UK
Printed in Great Britain by Ashford Colour Press Ltd

Contents

Figures

Tables

Acknowledgements

The writers who have tested and improved this book with their feedback are:

Jo Throup
Paula Greenlees
Rik Measures
Janet Murray
Jessica Borges Vaz
Katrina Ritters
Christine Lewry
Colin Morgan

About the author

Why listen to me?

The first novel I attempted was published by a major house. I wrote it as a single draft in the evenings over the space of nine months. Two more books followed and all may still occasionally be found in (charity) shops. Five more are in various stages of being accepted or rejected. Nevertheless, you've probably never heard of me. I'm not rich or successful, and to that extent I am one of the 75 per cent of published novelists who don't make a living from their books. That's the reality of the industry.

But I do make a living as a writer. As a corporate copywriter, I produce magazine articles, reports, adverts, training courses, letters, speeches, marketing materials, press releases, taglines, posters and internal communications strategies. People pay me to write things quickly and to order. They expect me to write exactly what they want, even when they're not entirely clear what that might be. It's my job to know.

I've also been a Creative Writing lecturer on an MA course that requires its students to produce a full-length novel as their final piece of work. That entails me teaching the essentials of craft and working over long periods with writers persevering to produce a complete polished draft. The lessons of this book are theirs as much as my own.

I'm motivated by a question I've been asking since I began seriously to write: 'Why did nobody ever tell me this stuff before?' If I'd known the things in this book ten years ago, I'm sure I could have started much earlier. Every writer should know them.

[McCreet] keeps a firm eye on structural machinery, giving us leisure to enjoy his stylistic sleights of hand.

Times Literary Supplement (2010)

James McCreet's splendid debut novel owes much to Charles Dickens's melodramatic style and subject matter. Victorian in both the setting and the telling, full of vividly depicted squalor and grotesquery, The Incendiary's Trail *begins with the murder of conjoined twins . . . Well worth reading.*

The Guardian (2009)

James delivers the most practical writing course I've ever experienced, and his eye for the positives and negatives of a manuscript is second to none. Which came first doesn't really matter: whether you are a planner using his blueprint up front, or a meanderer like me, using it as a guide for a second draft, I can't recommend him highly enough. His advice will ring in your ears.

Kim Hunter, MA student

New writers may baulk at the idea of organising their thoughts before they set out on their creative journey, but McCreet's suite of planning tools and narrative techniques help you to get one very important thing right from the outset: structure. These tools allow you to decide, chapter by chapter, on the structure that's right for your story. The end result is that you will never sit and stare at a blank screen.

Joe Field, MA student

I wanted to say a massive thank you for the part you played in my development as a writer. You've been one of the most influential tutors I've had at either undergraduate or postgraduate level. I can safely say that I wouldn't be at the standard I'm at, or have achieved the mark I got, without your involvement. I write better, plan better, push myself more, am more honest with myself, and am more disciplined because of what I've learnt from you.

RM, MA student

As a first-time novelist, I was experiencing many of the problems James discusses in this book. I was lost in a first draft, unsure how to make the story and structure work. He helped me realise that writing is only part of the novel-writing process and, with his support, I was able to repair my flawed first novel. By going back to the beginning, reconsidering the structure, and planning in more detail, I've been able to navigate my way through the process to completion.

Liz Champion, MA student

James has built a reputation among our readership as an uncompromising and valuable authority on matters of writing craft. His talent is in cutting through all the static, expressing clearly and concisely how writers can improve.

Jonathan Telfer, Editor, Writing Magazine

Introduction

Do we really need another book about writing?

As long as writers are having books rejected by publishers, yes. As long as writers are failing to finish novels, yes. As long as writers keep going through years of frustration, not being able to pinpoint exactly why they can't break through – yes.

Yes, because many of the books and courses and magazines and editing services already out there are telling only half the story. It's very easy to speak in generalities and abstracts. It's easy to give rules and hints and to suggest that following these will result in publication. This is, after all, why many such books are bought. They appear to provide answers, but what they so often fail to do is to capture the huge complexity of what writing a novel really entails – a complexity that's beyond hints and tips, beyond simple answers, beyond broad generalities.

Most aspiring writers are quite able to reel off 'the rules'. They've absorbed all the literature on the subject. They've work-shopped their writing and seem to know all there is to know about how to do it. And yet it still isn't working. Publication remains an apparently impossible dream. It's a paradox that naturally perplexes tens of thousands of writers, and it's my experience that genuine, serious, committed writers want to hear the *whole* truth. They want to know how difficult it really is and how best to approach the challenge. They don't want easy answers – they want the hard stuff. They want the *truth*.

Writing techniques *can* be taught. Better dialogue, better description, better grammar, 'showing and telling' – these are simple lessons that can be mastered with constant practice and detailed feedback. But they're only half the story because there's a tacit paradox at the heart of all writing endeavour. It is the rationale and the foundation for this book – the reason why we need another book on writing:

A novel takes more than writing.

The assumption among many first-time novelists is virtually automatic: I can write, therefore I can write a novel. It's not true. Deftness with dialogue, a clutch of competent short stories, a basting of workshop praise and possibly a qualification in writing are all useful, but not guarantees of a publishable novel – no more than the ability to make a table is the ability to build a yacht. The task is far, far more complex than it appears, as most people discover once they've begun.

Consider this: journalists and copywriters are professional writers. They produce words with a facility that many aspiring writers could only wish for, and yet there are numerous examples of them producing unpublishable or just plain bad novels. Sure, they might get published anyway, but if the industry shows us anything, it's that a well-known name on the cover is more important than literary competence. Which brings us to the crux . . .

This is not a book about 'writing'

There are countless other books and courses teaching you the essentials of craft. I'm assuming you can already write. You certainly shouldn't be attempting a novel if you can't. This book is about what you do next once you've grasped the basic skills of writing.

So many people begin a novel as if it were no more difficult than (or different from) a letter or short story. They believe that because they can write 1,000 or 5,000 words, they can write 100,000 words. No doubt they can. No doubt a carpenter can have a go at a yacht – but would you want to join him on a jaunt across the Atlantic in January?

My personal experience, and the experience of my students, is that most people who begin a first novel enter a morass of confusion and frustration than can take years to resolve. Multiple drafts follow, each one seeming to move the novel sideways rather than forwards. Storylines change. Chapters change position. Characters lapse. Some of these novels are simply abandoned in a fug of disillusionment. Others are sent off hopefully to publishers or agents and are rejected. Hope is not an active ingredient of a successful first novel.

Admittedly, the issue is often that the novelist has not yet mastered the basics of writing. Much more likely is the fact that the novel was poorly conceived. Indeed, I can say that every flawed first novel I've ever seen has suffered from exactly the same two errors. Both amount to the fact that the writers in question have not accepted or understood that . . .

A successful first novel is born before you write a word.

Writing is only one part – arguably the easiest part – of the process. The ability to write is insufficient in itself. A successful (and happy) novelist understands that writing is just one of a suite of technical and personal skills that must be developed. Among the others are: research, story-building, time management, editing and self-promotion. These are distinct skills. They don't come as part of a package with 'writing'.

How to use this book

My book is intended for writers who have reached a level of basic proficiency – those who can already write. It represents the next level for people who want to start their first novel, or who need to repair a flawed novel. You may already have been rejected by publishers and agents. Above all, the book is for writers who are serious about aiming at professional status and producing a finished novel. It is not a guide to improve general craft.

A number of processes are described here. They are not absolute rules. They do not represent a guaranteed path to publication. They may not apply to every conceivable kind of book. But they do offer many important ways to reconsider the thinking processes that come before writing (or, less efficiently, in a comprehensive edit). You might adopt some of them or all of them in whatever combination suits you. The most important thing is to be aware that they exist and that they can help you to produce a readable, publishable novel.

Many books like this end up being less about writing than about writing like the author. I may be guilty of this in some places. There is obviously no single way to write. We all choose our own paths, part of which is selecting which advice we take. Nevertheless, many thousands of writers do get lost before they find their way and most of them do so for the same reasons. At worst, this book will make you think about some of the practical ways a novel might be approached. At best, it might be the sword that cuts the Gordian knot of your frustrations as a first-time novelist.

Getting it wrong

The kinds of mistakes that first-time novelists make are typical and universal. Most are due to lack of foresight, planning and understanding of how a novel works, while the rest are caused by a specific misconception (dealt with in a moment). All are avoidable by employing the lessons of this book.

In my work as an MA lecturer, I've read and marked many complete first novels. Almost all of them suffer from the same kinds of flaws. Below is a list of these classic flaws – most of them made by writers who were totally unaware of the doomed path they were on. Towards the end of the book, we'll look again at the list and see with clarity exactly why each of these errors occurred and how they could have been remedied before a word was written. Do you recognise any of these mistakes from your own work?

Unclear narrative point of view

Who's telling us the story? Sometimes it's an omniscient narrator; sometimes it's a character – sometimes we're not sure. On one occasion, it's apparently a goldfish. A novel can be polyphonic, but only if consistently managed.

Summarising rather than narrating

The writer moves through a number of scenes, describing each one to the reader rather than letting the novel unfold. Essentially, there's a narrative stranglehold that won't allow characters to speak or episodes to develop. Another symptom of this is the rush to tell absolutely everything in the first 10,000 words, falling over oneself to describe character, location, theme and backstory so that story threads are hard to discern.

Halting structure

The scenes are well presented, but arrive disjointedly and perfunctorily as if in a queue. There's no sense of a connecting tissue between them – no flesh on the bones. Sometimes, the story jumps back and forth between backstory and main story, seeming always to be catching up or contextualising rather than moving forwards.

The premise is weak

The initial catalyst (the idea or primary scene) is insufficiently considered to carry the weight of the subsequent word count. The further we move from it without development, the weaker the novel is. Essentially, there's not enough narrative texture and story to keep the reader interested.

Diffuse and/or disconnected storylines

There are a number of storylines, but they seem to exist independently of each other as embryonic novels within the novel. This is fine if you want to encourage a degree of ambiguity or expectation, but not fine if they're not eventually reconciled or connected in any compelling way.

Occurrence unevenly distributed

There's a glut of action at the start or the end, but great wastelands of tedium in between. This naturally affects pace. There's nothing wrong with a languorous narrative flow, but it has to read as if you intended the effect and it has to be consistent.

Rushed or inconclusive endings

The climax seems to come out nowhere (in a bad way) or doesn't seem to fit with the pace and development of the narrative as a whole.

Do you write as a writer, or as a reader?

Many of the issues listed above stem from a paradoxical state of mind that acts as a barrier to the ability to write effectively. As writers, we're all readers. We've spent more of our life reading and studying books than we have writing them, and that creates a curiously inappropriate misconception.

We instinctively believe that because we can appreciate the finest and most subtle writing, we must also be able to produce it. We assume that the ability to spot the tiniest fault in other people's prose equates with the sense not to make those same mistakes ourselves. We believe that, because we've studied literature and have a critical sense, we are already somehow qualified as writers.

This is a powerful delusion.

Most first-time novelists stumble because they are writing as readers rather than as writers. It's a subtle confusion that goes unrecognised by most, but which is a crippling brake on progress. The writer-as-reader is schizophrenic because he is trying to fulfil two functions at the same time. His overwhelming experience is that of a reader, but his overwhelming desire is to be a writer.

Consider some of the psychological perspectives in Table 0.1.

Too often, the first-time novelist is the inadvertent reader in his own book. He writes to see what's going to happen next, hoping it will all work out (as it does when he reads). He writes his way into his own story as the reader reads into it. But if the writer is progressing blindly, if he doesn't know what will happen next, if he's waiting rather than dictating, if he's responding rather than influencing . . . who's managing pace? Who's managing consistency of occurrence? Who's in control?

Table 0.1 Writing as a reader or as a writer

The reader . . .	The writer . . .
follows the action of the story	dictates the action
is passive and waits to be told	knows what will happen before it's written and tells it
responds to seeded stimuli	creates a framework for reader engagement
can be blind – the plot shows the way	always sees beyond and behind
trusts the writer and has expectations	has a responsibility to deliver
is on a journey	has completed the journey before the reader
experiences the story	engineers the experience

This is one of the main reasons why writers get lost in their own novels. A reader can pick up a published book with no prior knowledge and just begin at page one in the certainty that everything will follow as surely as the pages are numbered. A writer can't. A writer has to understand the mechanisms of a novel *in advance* in order to write it. One can't produce and consume at the same time.

Your goal is to write as a writer. You must stand above your work and see it as a whole, even if the details are quite basic at the outset. You must plan a journey for the reader: the twists and turns, the surprises, the pleasure of language and character. Like a conductor, you're creating the score on which multiple parts will play out for a listener's discerning ear. When the reader feels excitement or fear or expectation, it's because you have orchestrated that experience for them.

> *The future for [the author] is then a blank page, whereas the future of the reader is two hundred pages filled with words that separate him from the end [. . .] The reader progresses in security. However far he may go, the author has gone further.*
>
> Jean-Paul Sartre (cited in Priest, 2002)

The hard way and the easy way

'Ah,' some might say, 'but many writers *do* just begin with an originating scene and make it up as they go.' This is true – many successful writers do write this way. But what they don't often reveal is how hit-and-miss, how frustrating, how lengthy and how ultimately inefficient this method is. Out of necessity, it requires multiple drafts, halts, repositionings and reversals. The professional writers I know who write this way produce up to twenty drafts of their novel, re-writing and rehashing until it seems they'll go mad. And then they have to hand it over to their editor, who inevitably gets to work on it so that further rewriting is necessary. You'd be surprised (and perhaps a little scandalised) how much of what you read is actually ordered by a publisher's editor rather than by the author.

And here's another issue: those successful writers who do make it up as they go along have usually refined some kind of system over the years that helps them. A system is necessary when you're producing numerous books. Ask them about their first book and they'll often tell you a story of unimaginable anguish. As a first-time novelist, your choice is simple: take the 'no-map' route and try your luck, risking every one of those pitfalls listed above (in addition to the colossal demand of time and concentration your novel requires), or follow the suggestions of this book and avoid all of them.

A simple test: if you are already able to produce publishable novels without fuss or stress, you don't need this book. If you're not yet at that stage, maybe it's time to try a new approach.

> *The first sentence can't be written until the final sentence is written.*
>
> Joyce Carol Oates (1989)

The stigma of planning

'Ah,' says the gentleman at the back wearing a battered Panama hat, 'but you take all the imagination and creativity out of the novel when you plan it like a military campaign. When you get lost on your journey, you discover places you didn't know existed and it enriches your trip.'

To which I reply: 'That's great, provided you're not on the way to A&E.'

It's sophistry to suggest that setting out without much of a clue equates with creativity, and that imagination alone is the touchstone of novel writing. Those student errors I listed earlier were not due solely to lack of imagination or technical ability. All were caused by lack of initial direction and foresight – a lack of prior knowledge about the mechanisms that make a novel work as a reading experience. More than that, the lack of direction curtailed the full flight of their imaginations because they were worrying so much about trying to make the story and structure work as they were writing it.

The point of planning is not to commit yourself to a rigid structure or story; it's to iron out problems before they occur, to provide a map of your novel, to provide yourself with the fuel and the tools to sustain yourself over many weeks, months or years of writing. It's about establishing a basic structural framework that will ensure success. This way, when you sit to write each day, you won't have to stare down the blank screen. You'll know what comes next and why. Your energy and commitment will remain high.

Moreover, you'll inevitably start to modify, flesh out and veer away from your plan as you go. This is not only inevitable, it's also desirable. As characters respond to situations, as better outcomes suggest themselves, you will amend your plan. Your preparatory work will have aided and guided your imagination.

Many writers seem to consider planning the very antithesis of creative writing. They say they like to start writing and 'just see where it goes'. This is perfectly fine when learning to write or exploring characters and themes. It's good practice. But the longer your word count, the more you will feel the lack of solid foundations. Rewriting will become necessary. Multiple drafts will become necessary. At some point, you're going to have to impose those structural elements that make a book readable. Why not do it before you write a word?

> *However great a man's natural talent may be, the act of writing cannot be learned all at once.*
>
> Jean-Jacques Rousseau (cited in Osborn, 2001)

The myth of writer's block?

Does it exist? In my opinion, it's a catch-all term too often used to label a host of other things. When many writers talk about being 'blocked', they've been deluded by the myth of the muse, of the creative spark, of 'talent'. They expect to sit at the keyboard and have words fall down upon them like literary manna every time. It doesn't usually work like that.

Perhaps you feel you've been blocked. You might recognise it as that feeling of inertia, of frustration and seemingly inability to get the words out. You sit for hours and tap out just a single sentence. But let me ask you a question: how often do you have the same problem with speaking? Does your mind ever go totally blank when talking to a friend? So blank that you're unable to speak for hours or days?

Professional journalists don't get blocked. Copywriters don't get blocked. Their jobs require them to produce words on demand, whatever their mood or the environment they find themselves in. Of course, a 1,500-word article is hardly comparable to a novel, but that's not the reason they don't get blocked. In fact, their apparent facility with writing is due to a number of factors.

The first and most obvious is practice. When you write every day, you get better at it. Then there's the attitude: it's difficult to be precious when your deadline is only an hour away. Perhaps most importantly, these writers work to a series of conventions and processes that structure the way their work is written.

A magazine feature, for example, has a number of accepted forms and precedents. Word counts and page layouts suggest formats. Interviews and research provide not only raw material but also narrative hints. The readership is known and duly catered for. The publication may have a style guide that dictates certain elements of language.

A novel should be no different. If you do your preparation and lay your foundations, you can sit down to write with the same kind of foresight. Know your readers, know your genre, know your structure, know your detail and your narrative lines, and there's no reason why you should ever be blocked. The reason we don't dry up while speaking is because we've developed a facility for it that's so instinctive we don't have to think. It's the same with writing. Practice does make perfect.

Certainly, there will be days when you're tired, when your kids are screaming, your partner bolshy, your nose running and your boss pushing you to a breakdown. On those days, you're entitled to feel disinclined to write or be distracted by life. But don't mistake this for something mystical called 'block' or even 'not being in the mood'. A professional writer should be able to write whether they're in the mood or not, just as a journalist can knock out an article to deadline even if their heart's not in it.

If you're someone who believes that you need a cottage by the sea or a sound-proofed subterranean cell in order to tackle your novel, you may not yet be ready to attempt it. If you believe that the benison of extra time will be the midwife to your opus, you will very likely be disappointed.

It's not writing that's difficult (if you can write) – it's knowing *what* to write. That's what this book is all about.

> *Professionalism probably comes down to being able to work on a bad day.*
>
> Norman Mailer (2003)

> *The term professional is not meant to imply a high standard of commitment and attainment: it means the pursuit of a trade or a calling to the end of paying the rent. I leave the myth of agonised creative inaction to the amateurs.*
>
> Anthony Burgess (1990)

A novel approach

Many creative-writing books and courses use exemplars from the world of literature: a snippet of James Joyce's free indirect voice, a page of Elmore Leonard's dialogue, a swatch of Angela Carter's description. As a teacher, I have mixed feelings about the approach.

A trainee chef doesn't learn how to cook a soufflé simply by eating one. You wouldn't want to take over the controls of a Boeing 777 after merely watching a video of a pilot flying one. Reading gives us this same false sense of security. We believe that, because we're able to identify a range of literary techniques in published work and the work of our peers, we can replicate them. This is patently untrue.

One of the paradoxes of the workshop is that people pick up others on exactly the same mistakes they're making themselves. How is it possible to *know* something and yet not be able to *do* it? The reason is that we learn how to write by writing as well as reading. Producing a piece of effective dialogue is compelling proof that you 'get it'.

The problem becomes even more difficult when we come to questions of structure. It's easy enough to study a page of dialogue for lessons, but a whole book has to be minutely studied to understand its structure. This takes time – time that most courses can't afford and which can bog down 'hints-and-tips' books with a lot of detail. The issue becomes yet more complicated when you understand that structure in published works is supposed to be invisible. Trying to find the joins and pick apart a seamless interwoven structure is difficult. It's about more than simple chronology or storylines – there are dozens of factors influencing how a particular structure was formed. And then there's the fact that there are few hard and fast rules. Novel structure tends to be organic. We can guess at what an author was trying to do, or how they managed it, but a guess isn't always much help.

Accordingly, you will find no extracts from well-known works in this book. You will, however, find some case studies from novels I've written. Not because my books are eternal monuments of literature, but because I wrote them and I know precisely how the structure was worked out. It seems to me that there can be few better practical examples of structure than from the author who possesses the original plot diagrams. By all means taste a soufflé, but then get yourself in the kitchen and burn a dozen. That's how you learn.

At the same time, I recognise that examples from one writer alone might seem prescriptive and restrictive. You may not want to write books like mine. I wouldn't want you to. Though it's impossible for me to know the exact processes used by other writers, I have also attempted to include in this book ways in which we might read other novels with an eye to understanding their structural elements. Specifically, I've chosen *Lolita* as a classic work of 'high literature' (and one of my favourites) that can stand as an example of how all novels – literary and generic – adhere to the same basic structural requirements. Please note: MULTIPLE SPOILERS.

Ultimately, a novel *is* a structural device. Even so-called 'plotless' or highly literary novels follow a discernible structure, otherwise they would be unreadable.

There are three rules for writing a novel. Unfortunately, no one knows what they are.

W. Somerset Maugham (2014)

1   Readiness

When are you ready to attempt your novel?

It's a good question, but evidently one that many writers don't give enough thought to. My first editor at Macmillan told me that 99 per cent of unsolicited submissions are from people who simply cannot write.

Stop for a moment and consider the implications of that.

Perhaps the most frightening thought is that tens of thousands of people have managed actually to produce enough words for a novel without ever realising they couldn't write. When we talk about the difficulty of getting published, we're really not talking about the vast competition of numbers – because only 1 per cent of unsolicited manuscripts are of the minimum standard! Of that lucky 1 per cent, a large proportion will have written uninspired, generic, poorly plotted or otherwise unmarketable material that won't earn a publishing deal.

When you look at it this way, you begin to realise that getting published is theoretically not that difficult at all. You only have to produce a well-written, marketable novel that stands out from the pile. If it takes so many months for agents or publishers to read your stuff, that's mostly because they're sifting through a mountain of mediocre or plain unusable stuff.

That's brutal. But it's true.

How is it possible that so many people have produced novels and submitted them without realising they were substandard? What led them to believe that their writing ability and the fabric of their material was in any way publishable? Blind hope explains a lot. Delusion affects many others. But I believe the main explanation is that many writers do not have a meaningful or practical appreciation of what it means to be proficient as a writer.

There are two broad strands to this truth. The first is a matter of basic craft: the handling of dialogue, description, characterisation etc. – even spelling and grammar. This kind of stuff is discussed in countless books, magazines, workshops, websites and classrooms around the world. It is teachable and learnable, but only through rigorous practice and serious feedback. The writers who don't 'get it' have possibly not put in the required work (the hours and years at the keyboard) or have failed to get the kind of objective feedback that every writer needs. There is no shortcut through it. Even if you have the willpower to produce a novel, it's almost certain to be rejected by a publisher if it lacks basic craft.

The second strand concerns the more complex requirements of idea, story, plotting, narrative, pace and overall structure. You might be adept at your basic craft, but your novel will be pretty much unreadable if you haven't also mastered these things. 'Being able to write' encompasses them, but they are too often glossed over in courses or books. The truth is that they are difficult to teach because it's necessary for students to produce tens of thousands of consecutive words in order fully to test these aspects of their novel-writing ability. I'd argue that at least 50,000 words need to be written and marked to give a realistic idea of proficiency in structure. That's just too much marking for most courses – even MAs.

The result is that most first-time novelists end up using their first novel as a testing ground for their skills rather than a showcase of them. In some ways, this is an admirable and necessary endeavour. It's a truism that one learns to write a novel only by writing a novel. This does not mean, however, that merely completing it is a sign of readiness. Most first novels are absolutely terrible and rightly remain unpublished. My own first book was not a novel but a travelogue set in Greece. I thought it was wonderful; no agent or publisher agreed. In retrospect, they were right.

In so many cases, therefore, the book that should be a pinnacle and summation of individual effort turns out to be a flawed and ineffective experiment. People don't like to accept this. They (rightly) place so much hope, ambition and effort into their first novel that they become almost incapable of seeing it as anything other than a masterpiece. This is the delusion mentioned above. The essence of their mistake (which was also my own) was to see their emergence as a writer represented by the production of a single book: their triumphant first novel. This is quite wrong and potentially destructive. Every writer should be constantly looking to the next book and the next. Each book is an exercise in improvement.

In other words, you should pretty much expect your first book to be unpublishable. True, this isn't much of a motivation to sit down and spend months writing it, but you should think of it as an apprenticeship. Approach it as a challenge, as an exercise. You can be justifiably proud even if you produce 100,000 words of very flawed material – you will have at least proved to yourself that you have the willpower. Maybe your second or third novel will be the one you send to a publisher.

This is the route most writers take, though usually inadvertently via a process of heartache and frustration, learning the hard way that the required standard is very much higher than what they are currently producing. Many give up. Who could blame them?

It needn't be *so* hard. My second attempt at a book (my first novel) was published – not because I am hugely talented, but because I had put in many years of practice to hone my craft and because I applied a process that made writing a novel both easier and more reliable. This book is that process.

How do you know if you can write?

Of all the questions the first-time novelist faces, this is the hardest to answer. How can you know? We've already seen that 99 per cent of people submitting their work to publishers are wrong in their earnest belief they can write. If you can't write, there's not much purpose in starting a novel. Surely there are some rules?

Certainly, there are some benchmarks to consider (see list below) and some broad measures of writing proficiency. You need a functional understanding – the ability to do, not just say – of dialogue, description, characterisation, narrative approach and the rules of grammar and punctuation. You'd be surprised how many first-time novelists have not mastered even these basic skills. Beyond this, certain elements of style and voice come into play: setting tone with sentence rhythm, games with vocabulary and advanced experiments in narrative approach. Such things can all be learned in classes, in books and through reading.

Still, how do you know when you've 'got it'? Is it enough if your friends say you can write? Your family? The people in your writing group? There's actually a very simple way to answer the question. Let's say you find an unexpected lump somewhere on your body. Would you trust your friends, your family or your peers to give you a reliable diagnosis? Let's say the camshaft on your car fractures. Would you similarly ask these people for their uninformed opinion and hand over the car to them for the weekend?

The answer, of course, is 'no' (unless your friends and family happen to number among them an oncologist or a mechanic). It's remarkable how readily we're willing to welcome the opinions of people when they're saying what we want to hear. What you *need* to hear as a writer is the unvarnished truth. Indeed, you should be looking for people to tell you what's *wrong* with your writing and exactly how you can remedy it. Praise doesn't help you improve. Criticism does.

Remember what we said at the start: you need to write as a writer and read as a writer. If your feedback is coming from people who read only as readers, they'll be able to tell you that the book is slow or boring or funny or OK. What they're unlikely to tell you is that you have an issue with narrative perspective, or that your sentence rhythm is repetitive, or that you need to vary paragraph length, or that you rely on cliché. These are the things you really need to know.

So who do you ask? Simply: somebody who is already proficient. Somebody who clearly and obviously knows more than you do. You ask a doctor about your lump, a mechanic about your camshaft, a writer/agent/publisher/lecturer about your writing. These people approach your writing as a patient or as a machine – not as a delicate piece of your personal sensibility. They have less interest in making you happy than your friends or family do. If your writing is broken or sickly, it needs fixing. No amount of glossing over the fact will fix it. No amount of praise from non-specialists will cure it.

When a genuine published writer, or agent, or publisher (or anyone else whose job it is to know the correct standard and whom you're not paying to be nice) tells you that you can write, you can be pretty confident you can write. You are ready to attempt a novel. The only other way to be sure is to write a novel and see if it gets published. The line between confidence and delusion is transparent – *something* has to be the arbiter, and that something is usually publication.

Self-publication, however, is not currently an indication of ability or readiness. Putting your novel on Amazon or other sites proves nothing except that you think your novel is good. I believe that any serious writer will be willing to drop their work into the bear pit of 'conventional' publication in the knowledge that it is good enough to triumph. It takes time, and the market can be both fickle and short-sighted, but when an agent or publisher is willing to bet their own income on your talent, you can feel confident that you're a 'proper' writer. You have proved it by winning over impartial and hard-hearted third parties. (Once you've proved yourself this way, feel free to upload your stuff and self-publish. Nobody can say you haven't paid your dues.)

All of this sounds evasive, I know. Understanding your own ability requires you to stand outside your work and see it as a stranger: as a reader rather than as a writer. When we look at other people's work in a workshop, we're reading as readers. When we read our own work, we're usually reading as the writer – blind to our own mistakes. It helps if you begin to think of yourself as a technician designing a 'user experience' for the reader. If you know how they should feel, when, and how this is achieved, it's easier to judge whether you've succeeded or not.

Ultimately, it's up to you who you ask and who you choose to believe. There are writers out there who live for praise and affirmation. They'll take it from anyone, careful never to show their work to someone who might see the serious flaws in it. A serious writer wants to hear what's wrong so they can put it right. A serious writer will understand that there is *always* something wrong, even if the book is published and earns universal acclaim.

The effective and proficient writer is his own harshest and most perceptive critic.

> *Do not take any 'advice' on how to write from anyone who has not written and published a significant piece of work.*
> Jeanette Winterson (2014)

Some indications you're proficient at your craft

- You understand 'showing v. telling' and can use both effectively.
- You maintain consistency of voice and pace.
- Your description is always commensurate to tone and purpose.
- Your dialogue says more than what's written.
- You know how to create engaging characters.
- You can correctly differentiate the uses of semi-colons, dashes and commas.
- You know that the position of a clause changes a sentence's emphasis.
- You no longer imitate your favourite writers.
- People say your writing sounds like you.
- You express yourself more easily in words than in speech.
- You'd rather write than do most other things.
- You no longer believe in mood or muse.
- You wake in the night with a better word.
- You're unafraid of the one-line paragraph.
- You can write while watching TV or on a train.
- You know that your 'best' work is often the first to be deleted.
- You love your dictionary like a close relative.
- You recognise cliché and avoid it.
- You write almost unconsciously.

(continued)

(continued)

- You know when you've written too much (or too little).
- You know there's no money in it, but still you persist.
- Your narrative unfolds automatically according to necessity of effect.
- You write almost every day because you feel compelled to.
- You have a voice (see below).
- Better writers than you say you're good.
- People pay you for your writing.

A writer is somebody for whom writing is more difficult than it is for other people.
Thomas Mann (cited in Earnshaw, 2014)

Your goal: objectivity

Knowing whether you can write is ultimately a case of being able to view your work entirely objectively – being able to read it as if you hadn't written it. How do you do this?

One way is to put your work away for a few months after finishing it and get on with something else in the meantime. It's amazing how clearly you see your work from a few months' distance, especially if you've been writing since you left it. Suddenly the immediate contexts and concerns of its origins are gone and only the text remains. Plus, constant writing makes us all better writers. You're a different writer when you read work you wrote in the past (which is why most published novelists can't bear to read their earlier work). I admit, however, that I'm too impatient to employ this method myself. I want to know that a book is finished and get on to new things. The occasional mistakes and infelicitous phrases in my published work show that my impatience has been rewarded.

Objectivity also comes from an internal 'criticism database'. When you've had enough years in workshops or showing your work to other people, you learn who gives the best feedback and you begin to anticipate what certain people will say. It's as if you hear their words before they even see the work and you re-read your stuff through *their* eyes: 'Oh, Barry would say this word is too pretentious . . . Sheila would pick me up on the voice there . . . Joe would say that's my flippancy coming through'. Even if you never see these people again, their critical faculties stay with you. It's *their* judgement you trust rather than your own.

Another path to objectivity is a healthy interest in the technical elements of the language. The more you know about syntax, grammar and punctuation, the better equipped you are to assess your work as a piece of functional prose. You begin to ask questions like: 'Why is this sentence so long? Does it add to the effect?' 'Why did I begin that sentence with a subordinate clause rather than a dominant clause?' 'Would this sentence read better with a full stop or with a semi-colon?' 'Would this paragraph have more impact in a different place?' It's no longer a question of how the prose *feels* – it's about immutable rules.

The same goes for dialogue, description, exposition, etc. If you know exactly *why* you decided on a particular approach (even in retrospect), you don't have to feel or believe that it is effective. You *know* it's effective because you created it with a very specific aim. You can argue it through. For example, a friend tells you that there's too much description at the beginning of Chapter 7. How do you know what 'too much' means? It might be that your friend just doesn't like description as much as another reader.

It's like cooking. If you use the correct ingredients in the correct quantities, combined in the correct way and cooked correctly, nobody can tell you that the meal is badly cooked. They can say only that they like or don't like it. The problem of writing objectivity is similarly solved in terms of ingredients and technique. If that description in Chapter 7 is intended to set up a scene, too much will kill the pace and anticipation rather than building it (just as too much boiling will ruin your vegetables). If the description is actually an elaborate metaphor, or is subtly revealing information that will prove important later, it's arguably not too much.

All such approaches depend on practice. Practice is the key to objectivity. Through endless practice, you develop an inbuilt sense of your writing's natural rhythm and you learn to judge it against its own standards. This takes us into the realms of voice.

> *We are all apprentices in a craft where no one ever becomes a master.*
>
> Ernest Hemingway (cited in Weis, 2010)

A note on voice

A lot is written about a writer's voice. Many writers aspire to it as a sign that they have reached a meaningful standard of proficiency. But what is a voice? How do you get one? Is it a sign that you're ready?

Your 'voice' is nothing more than your default writing style, evolved over many hundreds of hours of practice. Like your spoken voice, your writing voice is a natural and unconscious form of expression. You don't force it or nurture it (because then it's a posture or affectation) – it just develops.

The most important thing about a voice is not its distinctiveness or cleverness – it's the facility with which it allows you to write. When you have your voice, you no longer have to think and sit constipated at the keyboard. Your thoughts are almost automatically ordered by your voice as they come out in text. To this extent, your voice is an accumulation of your years of writing, reading, thinking and striving to make the sentiment on the page exactly the same as the feeling in your mind.

The more distinctive a voice, the more it approaches the mystical aura of 'style' – a truly unique textual personality that utilises exceptional craft to express an exceptional mind. There are some writers (Hemingway, Ellroy, Poe, Pynchon) who might be identified from a single sentence of their work. But there are others who are distinctive more by their ideas than by their voice. I'm not sure you can choose to have a style. Perhaps it just happens.

Not having a style is no barrier to success. Many of today's popular genre writers don't have powerful identifying styles, though they will have assured voices in terms of how they recognise and feel their own prose. Style, after all, can sometimes be a distraction if the plot is the driving impetus or if the characters need to jump off the page. Some of the best writers are utterly invisible behind the fabric of their work – a very difficult trick to pull off. Elmore Leonard is an acknowledged master of this. Such invisibility is still driven by a voice, however.

Is my voice discernable in my fiction? I have absolutely no idea. I was once told in a writers' workshop that my work was immediately identifiable whether I'd written sci-fi, comedy or tragedy. Was that my voice speaking? Or am I just very predictable? It's not something I want to think about. The essential thing is that the words come naturally – more naturally than speaking – and this is critical if you're working to a daily word count.

For the purpose of assessing levels of readiness to write a novel, voice is critical in one very significant respect. When you have a voice, you're able to read through your work and test it according to the rhythms and cadences of what you instinctively recognise as your own. When pace falters, when a clause jars, when an adjective doesn't gel, when a dash seems inferior to a colon, it clangs with wrongness. Having a voice makes you your own best critic because you learn to judge everything you write against your own consistent standards.

> *To gain your own voice, you have to forget about having it heard.*
>
> Allen Ginsberg (cited in Strickland, 1992)

Are short stories good training for a novel?

Short stories will certainly hone your craft. The distillation and close attention they require is good for your dialogue, your description and your appreciation of narrative. However, the short story also teaches you to think and write within a confined space – a frame – limited by word count and by the various strictures of the short-story form ('come in late, get out early' etc.).

A novel is an entirely different proposition. The narrative horizon is mostly beyond sight – you move towards it almost blindly, taking small steps. You can't really hold the whole thing in your mind at one time. A novel is very much like walking a tightrope into the mist. You trust that the other end is firmly tethered and you try not to look down. The two are quite different and separate skills.

Of course, there are many writers who produce novels and short stories with equal facility. I'm sure they would agree that their first novel wasn't much easier because they'd first written short stories.

Have you read enough?

Another rather obvious question, to which many people automatically answer 'yes'. The realistic answer is usually 'no'.

Some students confess to me that they don't really read anything beyond what's on the reading list, and barely even that. They draw inspiration from TV and cinema, which can indeed be instructive in terms of story and structure, but which help little with grammar and style.

Reading is certainly not a guaranteed or singular route to better writing. The assumption that a profound understanding of literature automatically promotes literary ability is shown to be false by the relatively few literature professors producing novels. Rather, reading is a way of honing the writing sensibility just as musicians train their ear by listening to music. The process is partially subliminal, teaching you fundamental truths about pace, dialogue, characterisation, etc. by endless variation and repetition.

But here's the thing: you have to do *a lot* of reading to internalise this literary sense. I believe you need to get to the stage that you've actively forgotten most of what you've read due to the sheer volume involved. You might not be able to remember any details of a particular Nobel Prize-winning novel you read twelve years ago, but it is in your head nevertheless – along with the other few hundred books you've subliminally absorbed.

An example. Sometimes when we're writing, an unexpected word will come to mind. Occasionally, it's a word we're sure we've never heard of, so we look it up in our trusty dictionary. Almost 100 per cent of the time, it turns out to be exactly the right word for the context. Where do these words come from? They come from some deep memory of reading – some part of the brain that exists not only to remember words, but also contexts, syntax and style. That serendipitous word comes from a novel I read last year or two decades ago. The title and the story have vanished, but some artefacts – like archaeological treasures – have remained in the cerebral strata.

It's not only words. Wide reading presents a remarkable encyclopaedia of techniques for you to absorb. James Joyce's compound adjectives, James Ellroy's staccato paragraphing, Kurt Vonnegut's sardonic brevity, Henry Miller's free-form flow, Franz Kafka's oddness, Edgar Allan Poe's openings, Herman Melville's voice, Vladimir Nabokov's wordplay, Anthony Burgess' vocabulary, Umberto Eco's metafiction, François Rabelais' lists, Shakespeare's neologisms, Ian Fleming's episodes . . . I wouldn't be the writer I am if I hadn't read these writers. There are hundreds more I can't remember, but who have added piecemeal to everything I know.

Emulation, however, is not the goal. Many first-time novelists will recognise the imitative urge. How many short-story writers find themselves copying Carver or Hemingway or Kafka? How many novelists begin their journey fixated on becoming the next J. K. Rowling, Stephanie Meyer or Terry Pratchett? This is another symptom of the writer-as-reader malaise. If you find that reading Charles Dickens or Ian Rankin brings on the urge to write like them, this may be a symptom that you haven't read enough. You haven't approached saturation. You haven't started to forget what you've read. You haven't begun work on your own voice.

This doesn't mean that there comes a time when you have read enough and can stop. Why would you want to? There's always more to learn and discover. In the last year, I've read Louis-Ferdinand Céline, Blaise Cendrars and Charles Bukowski for the first time. They may not change my voice or approach (as far as I know) but they have inspired me to aspire ever higher, to experiment more, to read more.

As we will see later, reading is also critically important in the formulation of ideas for your own novels. Knowing what has been written before is always handy to avoid inadvertent plagiarism, but the larger point is that imagination is primarily a skill of synthesis. Ideas seldom come from nowhere; they come from an accumulation of input. The more you absorb, the more you have to work with.

> *The difference between the almost right word and the right word is . . . the difference between the lightning bug and the lightning.*
>
> Mark Twain (cited in Camfield, 2003)

Reading as a writer

The previous chapter discussed writing as a writer. This also entails learning to read as a writer. When you read as a writer, you begin to be aware of the joins that the author intended to be seamless. You see the characters who were planted as catalysts; you see how storylines pivot on certain scenes; you see how passages of description act as mood-setters. In short, you see how each practical element functions.

It's useful to pick up the books of your favourite writers and dip into them as guides on technique. This doesn't mean *reading* them in any conventional sense, but examining them as exemplars. How long are their paragraphs? How often are there breaks in the narrative? How many lines of scene-setting do they allow themselves? How do they hook you at the beginning of a chapter or a sub-section? Such an approach requires you to maintain a writerly distance from the text because, if they've done their job properly, you shouldn't ever notice these things as a reader.

An example. I've recently started writing a novel that's something totally new and quite experimental for me in terms of voice, subject and approach. It's quite fragmentary and my fear is that the reader will stumble between these fragments, even though all are links in a carefully plotted sequence. I remembered reading something roughly similar almost two decades ago – a book by Patrick Leigh Fermor – and I went to buy a copy of it expressly for the purpose of checking how that writer had handled the same challenge. Reading as a writer, I was delighted to note that his work is even more fragmentary than my own, but never appears so to the reader because the continuity is carefully handled. I'd never noticed it as a reader.

Incidentally, many books are more fragmentary than we realise. There are not many writers who prolong a single scene over tens of pages (unless there's a good narrative reason). Chapter breaks and double-space breaks move the reader almost unconsciously between perspectives and scenes. The narrative momentum is always relentlessly forward. Taking a few books randomly off my bookshelf, the distance between the first line and the next break or chapter is:

Inside Mr Enderby, Anthony Burgess: 5 pages
Blood Meridian, Cormac McCarthy: 3 pages
Lolita, Vladimir Nabokov: 0.5 page
Journey to the End of the Night, Louis-Ferdinand Céline: 3 pages
A Tramp Abroad, Mark Twain: 4 pages
Hollywood, Charles Bukowski: 4.5 pages

What to read (and why)

It's easy to be prescriptive about reading lists. Too often, a friend or teacher suggests books that they feel are masterpieces but which you find dull or pretentious. I know this better than most – not many of my students are particularly enthusiastic about *Moby Dick* or *Lolita* (which are, officially, the two best books ever written).

We're all responsible for seeking out the books that are right for us. They might be the books closest to what we'd like to write, or the books we know we'll never be able to write. Curiosity is essential. Literary snobbery is limiting. I believe a writer should be interested in all varieties of writing – not only books. Ask anyone who professes a serious interest in music what they like. They're unlikely to say they listen solely to U2 or solely to Beethoven. They'll tell you they hear the best in everything.

You seldom find a writer who says the same thing. There's a snobbery implicit in writing that looks down on anyone who voluntarily reads a ghosted book by the latest model/actress, or a pulp spy novel, or whatever the latest mass-market phenomenon is. Ironically, many of the people who take such a stance may never reach that level of proficiency. Dan Brown has received blizzards of scorn for his prose, but few aspiring writers can match his narrative drive.

So, yes, read everything. Everything that's been published (by a publisher) has met a certain set of standards and been approved as marketable to a specific audience. A publisher has bet their own time and money on these books being a success. Everything can teach you something. You might not necessarily enjoy some of the books you pick up, and you may not finish them, but you'll have learned what not to do.

Also, start re-reading your favourites. Good books are written to be re-read. I've read *Lolita* four times, *Moby Dick* three times, *The Shipping News* four times and each of the James Bond books at least three times. Each re-read is a new experience because time makes you a different reader and a different writer. You see different things. *The Great Gatsby* was on my 'Top Ten' list for years, but my fourth reading of the book ruined it for me. My tastes had changed in the nine-year interim.

Here are a few areas you could explore to create your own reading list. You might feel inclined to skip this part if you think you're already sufficiently well read. But unless your reading typically extends to toothpaste packets and political speeches, I'd advise you to read on.

The old stuff

There can be few better measures of quality than how long a title remains in print. Daniel Defoe published *Robinson Crusoe* in 1719 and it's probably selling more copies each year than my own books do in 2016. Why? Because Defoe was a master storyteller who knew instinctively what his audience wanted – not just an eighteenth-century audience, but a human audience.

That was back when the novel was first becoming known as the novel. Before that, there were a few millennia of other stuff. Defoe would have been familiar with Homer's *Odyssey* and *Iliad*.

The English translation of *1001 Nights* was also available from 1706 – that compendium of ancient Persian, Arabic and Egyptian tales that can still be seen regularly in film and TV today. All are stories that have captured the imagination of children and adults for hundreds or thousands of years. If you could extrapolate even a strand of that narrative essence, you'd already be at a great advantage.

We assume that modernity gave birth to literary experimentation. *Ulysses* is often cited as the breakthrough book of Modernism. We talk about Post-Modernism and (De)Constructionist texts as being solely twentieth-century phenomena. We talk about *Lady Chatterley's Lover* being a watershed in the handling of literary obscenity and censorship. But I direct your attention to the bawdy humour of Geoffrey Chaucer (1343–1400), the inspired, obscene imagination of François Rabelais (1494–1553), the sprawling imaginative canvas of Miguel de Cervantes (1547–1616) or Laurence Sterne's unique *Tristram Shandy* (1759).

Such works, and countless others like them, are not only the foundation for pretty much everything that's been written since, they are also often much bolder than we imagine in their experimentation with style and narrative. Rabelais was one of the most intelligent and well-read men of his era, but he is not above providing us with a three-page list of adjectives to describe testicles. Surely that alone is an incentive to read ever further back.

The King James Bible

Many words have been written about the language of this book. It is undoubtedly part of the DNA of all western literature and contains stories that have gone beyond mere narrative to become metaphor and context to centuries of writing.

Just dipping in can be an exhilarating experience. Try Ecclesiastes or Revelation and be stunned by the prose. Read from the start of Genesis and see the world begin, as well as phrases you've read a hundred times before elsewhere. Reading this version of the Bible is like hearing an echo through all writing. It is a text imbued with all the majesty you would expect from a book that aims to encapsulate the meaning of life itself.

At the same time, it captures the purest essence of storytelling. We all know the story of the Good Samaritan, or Noah, or Moses, but going back to the source material reveals just how succinctly these stories were told. It's sometimes just a matter of lines, with not a word wasted. Perhaps this why the stories are so memorable: they are constructed intuitively and designed to be told and re-told.

The canon

We're talking about the average university literature reading lists, covering books from the eighteenth to the twentieth centuries. You know the kind of thing. The point is that these books have been chosen by posterity (and by generations of readers) as great, so there must be something in them. Some you'll love; others you'll despise. Personally, I could never get on with George Eliot or Henry James. I find Dickens often mawkish and tedious. But at least I've tried.

From my late teens to my early twenties, I went through a phase of reading as many Nobel prize-winners as I could. Some were already known to me (William Faulkner, Thomas Mann, Ernest Hemingway, Albert Camus) while others were not (Naguib Mahfouz, Knut Hamsun, Henryk Sienkiewicz). I found some of them profound – even life-changing in the sense of how I imagined my own existence. Others I abandoned as too heavy. I'm sure they all did me some good.

Contemporary

It makes sense for the first-time novelist to keep an eye on what's being published right now. Indeed, many courses include a unit on just this kind of writing, reasoning that the contemporary market is what new writers need to be aiming at. There is certainly some truth in this, but it's not as straightforward as it seems.

One shouldn't confuse 'writing for the market' with 'chasing trends'. When one writer has success with a series about boy wizards, you can be certain that 10,000 other writers will produce something very similar. This creates a flood of very samey work over the desks of agents and publishers, with the result that the trend soon becomes passé. More importantly, the turnaround that most novels require for writing and publishing means that whatever the trend was when you started writing is unlikely to be a trend when the book comes out. By all means keep track of the market, but don't try to second-guess it.

If there's one thing publishers want more than what's already selling well (crime, for example), it's something that the publishers haven't got: something new, something original. To this extent, a contemporary book is whatever publishers decide to publish now. You might have written a novel based on the journal of a fifteenth-century explorer. If it's good, it'll get published.

Indeed, it's worth remembering that the books being published now were very probably influenced by books being published at least twenty or thirty years ago. Should you be reading the book that's just come out, or the ones that inspired it? The obvious danger of too much focus on contemporaneity restricts or prevents the advantage of absorbing the lessons of the canon. Just look at the pop music industry, which – in its ever-more frenzied thirst for quick profits – is releasing songs with the longevity and heritage of a mayfly. Everything is about riding the wave of current trends. Will the songs of Justin Bieber be played and enjoyed in thirty years? Are they being played at the time of publication?

Yes, you should be reading some of whatever is being reviewed this weekend. But reading *Lolita* or *Moby Dick* or *Slaughterhouse 5* or *Catch-22* will change your life.

Cinema

Too often overlooked by writers, films provide an excellent training ground in so many narrative techniques. A film – like a shark – has to keep moving to stay alive, so everything has to be designed for the viewer's point of view. A screenplay is written for the camera's eye, telling it where to look and what to see. We understand a character from his actions as much as his words. We understand tension as much through the edit as through the script.

Observe how and when scenes change, how they are juxtaposed, how long they are and what purpose they're used for.

Observe how the first few seconds of screen time for each character manage to sum them up, even if they don't speak. Observe how assumptions and expectations are woven into the plot to keep us watching.

Pulp and genre

It was only after I'd had two novels published that I began to realise my debt to the hundreds of disposable thrillers I ingested in my teens. These are the kinds of books that are usually derided for their cardboard characters, their predictable storylines, their gratuitous violence and explicit sex. The 1960s and 1970s saw an explosion of this sort of thing: Harold Robbins, Arthur Hailey, Desmond Bagley, Jackie Collins. I was really only a child when I started reading them, but I consumed them compulsively. I became briefly obsessed with a long-running American spy series ghost-written under the name Nick Carter.

Genre fiction is the hardiest of literary forms. Poe kicked off the detective/crime genre in 1841 and today it's the best-selling sector of the market. Romance is not far behind, with imprints set up especially to cater for voracious readers of gentle ravaging. Sci-fi is often derided by literary snobs, but has proved to be an absolute mine of ideas for Hollywood. At east one sci-fi writer has his own religion.

The point is that these books live and die on story. Maybe the writing isn't always top drawer, but they have pace, conflict, cliffhangers and scenarios designed to keep you reading all night. They sell in their millions because they give their audience exactly what they want – the opposite of the literary giant who writes only for himself.

Whatever kind of book you want to write, you need to keep your audience in mind. You have to give them at least a little of what they need to stay engaged. The stalwarts of pulp and popular fiction have gained mastery of this kind of narrative and they remain richer reading experiences than ever. You might be disdainful of someone like James Patterson, but allow yourself to read one of his books just to see why millions of people can't resist them.

Foreign bodies

Our university courses tend to steer us towards the traditions that built our immediate cultures, with the result that we read far less foreign writing than we might. Translation quality remains an important arbiter of how good our experiences are, but there's a world of influence to be found in stepping outside our own cultural frame.

Take French literature as an example. Reading Gide, Céline, Sartre, Camus, and Cendrars is likely to give you a whole new perspective on twentieth-century writing: one that seems somehow more raw, more challenging, and often more liberal in tone than what British or American writers were producing at the same time. These are influences that any writer can surely benefit from.

Go back a bit further and see how Hugo, Verne, Maupassant and Dumas demonstrate a mastery of popular storytelling than can make English novels of the same period seem verbose and turgid in comparison. Is it any surprise that the French embraced Edgar Allan Poe before most of the English-speaking world did?

Plays

We might study plays at school, but we seldom go back to them in later life. We should, because the playwright offers many lessons in how to make dialogue work. While many aspiring writers weigh down their dialogue with excessive description or pointers for the reader, the playwright uses only the characters' words. We understand the character through what they say and do, not what we're told about them by an omniscient voice.

Shakespeare is always worth revisiting. He's a totally different read outside the classroom or lecture theatre – a writer who was in love with language and who played with conventions while never straying from what his audience wanted. He was the ultimate professional writer, turning a popular form of entertainment into eternal art. I occasionally read *Macbeth* just before beginning a new novel; it recharges my literary batteries.

And let's not forget the ancients, whose plays are still being performed 2,500 years after they were written. Aeschylus, Euripides,

Sophocles, Aristophanes wrote plays of such plangent humanity (or ludicrous satire) that they – like the Bible and the 'old stuff' – form a foundation for most western writing. Yes, they represent art of the highest order, but these playwrights were also often writing to win competitions and popular support. They married technique with a constant attention to giving the public what they wanted.

Speeches and manifestos

When a politician or a priest or an activist stands before a crowd, they have a few minutes to engage the crowd. Not only engage, but also persuade, convince and energise. The argument must be clear and memorable. The language must suggest a tone and capture a feeling. Seldom are such demands put on a piece of writing.

Rhetoric, or course, is an ancient art, and the techniques used by modern politicians are largely the same as those used in classical Athens. Have a look at Martin Luther King's 'I have a dream' speech, or Barack Obama's 'Yes we can' or Terry Waite's speech on being released from captivity. Here were words to change history. If we, as fiction writers, can learn some of the rhetorical techniques used by orators, we can add some of their power to our prose.

Random and accidental

There are some books you would never read, either because you've never heard of them or because you consider them anathema to your delicate mind. Sometimes, however, you find yourself in a situation where you're inclined to have a go.

I'm talking about books found on a bus, books in the meagre 'library' of a foreign hotel, books that are so cheap in the charity shop that it would be foolish not to buy them. I once picked up a book from a market stall in Krakow's central railway station because it was the only English title I could see. It was called *Compulsive Incest* and was a pornographic novel produced cheaply in New York sometime in the early 1980s. Needless to say it was as grotesquely explicit as it was badly written, but it was also brilliant fuel for any future parody I may choose to write. Certainly, I would never have gone looking for it in a bookshop in England.

Random reading leads us out of our comfort zone into the realm of bad romance, celebrity memoir and bizarre sub-genres. These are areas where our imagination may never have ventured – areas in which unexpected ideas may be lurking. The more we absorb, the more we have to work with

Journalism

Journalists have fewer words to work with. News stories in particular have to get straight to the point and reveal all the information in the most concise manner possible. The skill of this kind of writing is in immediately delivering what the reader wants and then adding supporting detail later. It's a hierarchy of needs: the headline, the standfirst, the first sentence and then the rest. How do you structure the story to meet this pattern?

Features are no less structured. You need to hook the reader with an idea or a bold statement and hang the rest of the narrative flow from that 'peg'. It's a story in the most elemental sense: one step organically flowing into the next so that the reader is carried along. Apparently so simple on the page, it's actually a complex and difficult thing to get right.

Perhaps even more critically, the journalist exemplifies a microcosm of this book's entire rationale. Everything he writes is driven by a clear understanding of audience and structure. A news story cannot afford to ramble. An article fails if it has a lengthy preamble as the writer 'gets into it'. The journalist must know from the first critical sentence where the story is going to go.

Commercial copy

We're surrounded by words that we barely register at a conscious level. Advertising hoardings, toothpaste tubes, cereal packets, health and safety warnings, furniture-assembly instructions and charity-fundraising junk mail – it's a non-stop blizzard of stuff. Why do we not seem to notice it? Because it's disguised.

Superficially, it's used purely as a communication tool, but there's always an agenda. We may not notice the writing, but we usually get the 'message' (if the copy is good).

It's easy and natural to pick up a novel or magazine and read it. The writing within has been designed expressly for your entertainment. But the writing on these other, commercial and informational, spheres has been designed even more explicitly to put ideas in your head or tell you how to do something. They succeed or fail on the effectiveness of the meaning *between the lines*.

There are lessons for all of us in the exquisite subtleties of commercial copy. Every sentence, every word, every punctuation mark has been considered according to its desired effect on a target reader. If there's even a flicker of confusion, doubt or boredom, it's 'game over'. Harnessing these techniques can only make your hold over your reader even stronger.

> *Far more thought and care go into the composition of any prominent ad in a newspaper or magazine than go into the writing of their features and editorials.*
>
> Marshall McLuhan (2003)

A word on NOT reading

Reading is important. But there's also a danger of becoming so lost in the labyrinth that you never get the freedom or time to find your own individual voice. The flood of words can overwhelm you, distract you and even create a crippling sense of inadequacy. How could you ever measure up to these literary giants?

There may come a point when it's time to stop reading for a while. For me, the decision was fortuitously involuntary. I lived abroad for seven years, during which time it was often difficult to find books in English. I picked up a few here and there, but mostly I just wrote. The effect was quite interesting: suddenly that cacophony of literary influence I'd been hearing all my life became muted. A void emerged and I felt able to fill it with what I wanted to say. My own voice began to develop because it was the strongest one I was hearing. Sequestered from the world of reading, I felt the words coming from the *inside* for the first time.

It's difficult to know when, or if, it's time to stop reading for a while, but it might turn out to be the catalyst you need. Books will be waiting for you when you come back. They might even offer more once you've changed your perspective on writing.

> *I think it can be tremendously refreshing if a writer has something on his mind other than the history of literature so far. Literature should not disappear up its own asshole, so to speak.*
>
> Kurt Vonnegut (2010)

The right attitude

It will have become clear by now that readiness is not necessarily the same as willingness. We've already seen that you shouldn't expect your first novel to be the first that gets published. We've noted that your desire to write might not yet equate with your proficiency as a writer. These are hard pills to swallow, but they are essential considerations.

Writing a novel is one of the most difficult things you may ever attempt. It requires not only a vast amount of time and practice in getting the basics right, but it also demands a superhuman effort of will in overcoming doubt, maintaining momentum, staying patient and withstanding the lacerating criticisms you secretly know are right on the mark. It's a masochistic process and there has to be pleasure if you're ever going to see it through.

Having the right attitude before you begin your novel means understanding and accepting the challenges you face. It's all up to you. Nobody else is going to write your novel for you, no matter how much help and encouragement they provide. Often in my initial MA seminars, I ask students why they've come on the course. Answers include:

    'I need someone to give me deadlines to make me write.'
    'I need someone to give me a structure to learn.'
    'I just can't find the time to write.'
    'I think being among a community of writers will help me.'

All are legitimate reasons for doing such a course, but I'd question whether such answers show readiness actually to begin a novel. The writer who is ready to begin their novel already has all the drive they need. They *make* the time. They set and keep their own deadlines. They've generally moved beyond the need for workshopping. All they lack are the few 'extra-literary' skills needed to tackle the challenge (the skills outlined in this book).

That's not to say, however, that the course won't help them towards the goal of becoming more competent writers, which in turn will make them ready to begin their novel. This is a realistic expectation from such a course. In my experience, the writers who get published shortly after completing an MA are almost always those who were 90 per cent ready before they began. For the rest, I'd expect between two and five years of hard graft after the course has ended before a novel begins to look possible.

On the next page is a diagram describing the factors that contribute to writing mastery. You'll notice that talent and imagination are not featured. That's because these are not distinct or pre-existing elements – they grow out of the other factors.

Knowledge refers to what reading has given you, as well as the craft that you've picked up from books and classes.

Experience is nothing more than the life you've lived, which is instrumental in your voice but which you can't do much to change unless you follow Orwell and Hemingway in volunteering for the Spanish Civil war, or become homeless in Paris like Henry Miller.

Feedback, as mentioned above, is the essential input you need from better writers than you. The more specific, the better.

Luck is just what it says: an undeniable but unwilled factor that may or may not help you out.

Failure is the leavening agent that most of us fear or avoid, but which is necessary for us to improve. Nobody can sit and

Figure 1.1 Factors contributing to writing mastery

write a publishable first novel without initially writing something inadequate, so we have to embrace failure and see it as a natural part of the process.

Practice is, of course, the only way to hone your craft and find your voice. We learn to speak by talking. We learn to write by writing.

By **attitude,** I mean the lucid understanding and acceptance of what the task involves and the willingness to undertake it. The challenge will inevitably require you to fight against the weaknesses in your character, to seek and reinforce your strengths, to struggle daily with this thing that obsesses you. You must have confidence in your ability. Failure to have the right attitude will see you falter at the first step or give up before you reach the typical first-novel watershed of about 10,000 words.

Some signs that you might have the right attitude

- You're willing to get up early or work late to get it written.
- You're willing to set a rigid daily word count and adhere to it maniacally.
- You have a list of priorities and your novel is just below sleeping or eating.
- You know that you should never look back – just keep writing forwards.
- You know that small, regular steps will get you where you want to be.
- You accept that it all might be rubbish so far, but you carry on regardless.
- You write despite your mood.
- You'd rather write two bad books this year than spend the next decade on a mediocre one.
- You welcome an unexpected thirty minutes to write on a train or in a café.
- You know that this book might fail, but you already know what the next could be.
- You fight fear with self-willed confidence.
- In the end, you're really only writing for yourself.

Writing is finally about one thing: going into a room alone and doing it . . . The haunting demon never leaves you . . . that demon being the knowledge of your own terrible limitations, your hopeless inadequacy, the impossibility of your ever getting it right.

William Goldman (2010)

I started writing when I was twenty, and my first book came out seventeen years later.

David Sedaris (n.d.)

Readiness to write a novel is usually attained by
cessful novel. It might not be your first or ever
The point is to develop the objective measures by which you re
ognise that your novel is genuinely successful. This comes with
practice, but also with the conscious development of processes
that allow you to go beyond your 'gut feeling'. Guts can be notoriously misleading – they say a lot. But it usually stinks. You're
ready when you've done it, but you're also ready when you correctly recognise you've done it.

The safety net of preparation

All of these things – the craft, the voice, the reading, the *not*
reading, the attitude and the practice – are necessary elements
of readiness. Unfortunately, many of them take a long time to
acquire. And even when you have them, you're still facing a very
difficult task.

That's where preparation comes in. The rest of this book lays
out the practical steps you can take to develop a process that
makes novel-writing easier. Many things dictate whether you're
ready to write your novel, but perhaps the greatest measure of
readiness is that you are prepared and you understand how a
novel works.

Preparedness minimises doubt, aids willpower, structures your
efforts and allows you to fit the novel into the rest of your life.
With preparedness, you are not the writer-as-reader. You should
not get lost inside your own book. You should not see the months
and years slide by without any clear indication of progress.

Readiness in summary

- You're ready when you're genuinely proficient at your craft.
- You're ready when you're your own best and harshest critic.
- You're ready when you've absorbed a wealth of reading.
- You're ready when you understand the scope of the challenge.
- You're ready once you truly know you've already done it!
- You're ready when you're prepared.

Readiness exercises

- Go to a second-hand bookshop (if you can find one) and buy a book at random, or of a genre you've never read before. What can you learn from it?
- Start *really* reading the copy on the back of cereal packets, washing-powder boxes and shampoo bottles. Note how the language is used (vocabulary, sentence length, punctuation, etc.).
- Jot a list of things that groups or individuals have said about your writing. Add to this list with each new piece of feedback you get and take action on the things that make sense to you. When you find you're not getting any new or helpful feedback, it's time to look for new critics.
- Set yourself a realistic word limit for each day and stick to it no matter what, even if you're just experimenting. In time, you'll start to increase the amount of words. Such discipline is necessary.
- Volunteer to produce writing for blogs or websites or magazines, even if you're not getting paid. The deadlines, word counts and structural requirements of commercial writing will make you a more natural and conscious writer (no longer requiring assistance from the fickle muse).
- Go back to a favourite film and make some notes as you watch. How are characters introduced? How many different scenes are there and what does each scene do? Time the film and mark the moments when key events occur. You'll see all sorts of patterns emerging.
- Find a list of the 'Top 100 novels of all time' (or similar) and choose half a dozen of the ones you've heard of but not read. Read them!
- Start a diary/journal and write about your daily thoughts or experiences. Show it to nobody. A journal is an excellent way to encourage a voice because it's something you write for no reader other than yourself. You can write without fear. Attempt to capture exactly what happened and how you felt.

2 The idea

Few things are as bewildering, as deceptive or as elusive as the so-called 'big idea' that writers expect to kick-start their novel. So many misconceptions surround the concept. In my experience, an insufficiently coherent idea is usually the primary cause of a first novel faltering and ultimately failing.

The main issue is a misunderstanding of exactly what an idea for a novel consists of. All ideas are not born equal, and what initially seems to be a good idea is often little more than the tiniest seed of a novel – merely a germ that may even disappear once the work is underway.

Let's be absolutely clear: your book isn't going to get published only because it's well written. Writing ability is a given. Your book is going to get published because of the idea, which translates ultimately as the story you're pitching. When you approach a publisher, they don't want to hear about your innovation with sentence structure or how you've interwoven your themes. They ideally want to hear something that already sounds like a marketing pitch. 'It's about a holy man who lives in a well.' 'It imagines what would have happened if Marilyn Monroe had lived.' 'It's a Young Adult novel set in a camp for exceptional singers.'

The idea is king. No doubt you've read bestsellers which you think are absolutely awful. Many of them *are* absolutely awful. I've read books by minor celebrities that have made me weep for the English language. These books were obviously bought and sold on their ideas alone (and on the perceived celebrity of their 'writer'). There's no reason why good writing and a good idea can't be happy together, but the idea is what sells the book.

This chapter looks at what constitutes a workable and market-able idea. It interrogates where ideas come from and how an idea is built into such constructive elements as theme, character and story. Every novel must have a starting point, and it must be a sound foundation if the work is to survive.

> *A book is simply the container of an idea – like a bottle;*
> *what is inside the book is what matters.*
>
> Angela Carter (2012)

But it's a true story!

Every writer has lived under some delusion about the value of a particular idea. These are the misconceptions that cause profi-cient writers to embark upon a doomed journey into a novel that isn't going to work. Here are some I've suffered from myself, and which my students occasionally embrace:

Some common misconceptions about ideas

- Once you've had your 'big idea' you can just sit and write the whole novel.
- The 'big idea' is the same thing as a plot.
- It's a true story, so it must be good.
- It's autobiographical, so the narrative flow will be clear.
- I can begin with a 'style' or a 'feeling' and the story will just come.
- I know the first chapter, so that's sorted.
- If I want it enough, inspiration will follow.
- Everyone has a novel in them.
- It's totally original.
- It's about a wizard/vampires/mummy porn – it'll be a sure-fire hit.

What is an idea for a novel?

It depends who you ask. For the purposes of this book, it might be best to divide the answer in two. There's the idea as far as the publisher is concerned, and the idea used by the author as the directing force behind the novel's construction. The former is concerned with the book as a finished, packaged entity; the latter is needed as a foundation from which to build the book. There may ultimately be very little in common between the two.

As a writer, you have to consider both sides of the equation. You need to give the publisher what they need while also serving your own purposes. You need to keep your eye on a future marketing pitch and a target audience before you've written a word, but you also need to nurture the idea as something unique and personal to yourself. You have to cherish it and watch it grow. It will be your baby for as long as you're writing it, but then you hand it over, they put it in a suit, comb its hair and send it out to trade. It's your duty to imbue your baby with all the integrity, hardiness and good sense it's going to need out there on the street.

What do publishers and agents want?

They're not entirely sure, but they know it when they see it. This is not particularly helpful.

William Goldman's comment about Hollywood, that 'nobody knows anything', might equally be applied to the publishing industry. Yes, they know quality when they see it. They can spot a good writer. But it's very tricky for anyone to predict public taste or trends. Often, a book that everyone previously thought was terrible will become a bestseller. There are endless stories of books turned down by multiple agents which then go to sell a million as e-books.

As mentioned above, it's difficult to chase trends. A writer might be lucky if the book they wrote a year ago turns up in the slush pile just as a similar trend is taking off, but you can't plan for this. At one point, publishers might have been looking for a 'Richard-and-Judy-style' book, or a 'book-club-style' book, but these are just pinning-the-tail-on-the-donkey stabs at popularity.

The amount of competition means that a successful book these days has to be something that stands above the rest: the same as what people already like, but different.

Nevertheless, there are some things you can bear in mind while coming up with your idea. It's easy to be cynical about box-ticking, but we're all readers ourselves, too, and there are certain things we all like.

Indications of publishing potential

- Genre fiction
- A projected (or completed) series
- 'Literary fiction' as apposed to 'literature'
- Being really famous already
- A gripping, page-turning narrative
- An interesting subject area offering added value
- Great writing matched by lucid structure
- Something new the market's ripe for
- A broad demographic experience
- A rare demographic experience
- Piggybacking off another book/cultural phenomenon
- Something unique and brilliant – a new paradigm.

Writing only for the market?

It might be tempting to attempt a book that ticks all the boxes, but such things tend to have numerous precedents in failure. Hollywood's reputation for a fatal love affair with the sequel or copycat films need hardly be cited. When we write a book to a formula, we too often risk losing the key ingredients of what makes a book work: passion, individuality, personality, voice. You might be able to write such books and even make a living from them – but would you enjoy yourself? Would you be challenged and grow as a writer? It would end up as a production line.

Here's a confession, however. Before writing my first published novel, *The Incendiary's Trail*, I drew up a list of elements that seemed to feature in all of my own favourite books.

Clearly, these elements had contributed not only to the books' long success, but also to their being published in the first place. The process also allowed me to understand (and therefore to write for) a possible audience.

My intention was to use this list as a guide – even a formula – to direct the writing of my first novel. There would be no compromise in style or approach, however. This was never intended to be a set of guidelines I would slavishly follow. I was determined to write it in exactly the way I wanted to. I was giving 'them' what they wanted, yet keeping the rest for myself.

The book *was* published, but has not (yet) become a worldwide bestseller. You may decide for yourselves where I made my mistake. I've lost the original list, but it must have looked something like this:

What my readers want

- Memorable episodes
- Distinctive characters in an ensemble cast
- A compelling, well-structured plot
- A dramatic opening
- A climactic ending
- A cinematic feel (for potential adaptation)
- Multiple plot strands
- Historical setting as added value
- Evocative period language and vocabulary
- A strong genre connection
- First in a projected series
- Something long enough to justify the cost.

Most of it seems pretty obvious now. These are not ideas in themselves – not in the sense of catalysts for a particular story – but they are interesting considerations of approach and of important elements that should stand behind any ideas you have for your book. It's good to think about what *type* of book you're going to write as you think about what book you're going to write. Such thoughts will prove essential later when you get to plot and structure.

Additionally, if you have these kinds of questions in mind as you work on your own idea, you will already have a framework in place on which to build character, story and theme. When you've identified an audience, or genre or narrative form, you're in a better position to work on your idea.

My list was created for a work of commercial fiction. Would there be a different list for a more literary work? Look again at those bullets – how many would you expect *not* to find in literature? If your idea is determinedly aimed at the literary end of the market, you may want to make a similar but slightly different list. It might look like this:

What my readers want (from literature)

- Complex thematic concept
- Distinctive style and voice
- Innovative/compelling narrative perspective (unreliable?)
- Provocative structural elements (narrated in reverse?)
- Detailed understanding of another world/context
- Originality – a work *sui generis*
- Challenging, experimental language
- A work that acknowledges a wider literary heritage
- The kind of thing that might win a literary prize.

It's a different list, but it's still the kind of thing that provides direction for the development of your idea. You know what you want to achieve in advance, so you can work more clearly towards collecting the required ingredients.

Write what you know?

This traditional piece of advice is simultaneously wise and misleading. The fact is: all writers write what they know. Every character, situation and sentence structure comes ultimately from our knowledge and experience of the world. It's impossible for us to write things we don't know. Our very imaginations are accumulations of reading, writing, culture and personal interactions.

However, it's dangerous to imagine that our knowledge alone is enough to create a novel. At best, it will provide characters, situations and a storyline or two. For example, John Niven's darkly excellent exposé of the music industry *Kill Your Friends* is based on his own experience as an A&R man. All of the detail rings true (no matter how extreme) but he has not simply regurgitated the anecdotes of a career. He has had to impose character arcs, plot, a story, a narrative approach and structure on his book. All of this is artificial.

Or take my own (currently unpublished) book *Holiday Nightmare*, which is based on my time working as a holiday rep in Greece. My experience alone was not enough to create a novel. There was no story – just a series of events. My perceptions from that time were all from my point of view. In order to make it into a novel, I would have to make my experience just one small part of a wider and more multi-layered book. Everything I *knew* would have to become background veracity to the artifice of structure.

Many first-time novelists are caught out by the 'write what you know' trap. They assume that experience of something always equates with knowledge, but there is always more to know. Your experience has to become the reader's immersive experience by way of a structured story. You can't just relate it as it happened because experience is subjective, unstructured and often illusory – you have to drop the reader into it in a way that makes sense to them. In failing to do a little research or add layers of creative dimension, you end up simply narrating 'what happened'. The reality gets in the way of the fiction. This is especially the case when writing in first person (even as a character).

This was certainly my own experience as a young writer. The intense focus on the self and one's own experience can be a trap. One has to learn to stand outside the material and view it with cold objectivity. For this reason, one of my initial epiphanies as a writer came when I chose to write only novels whose subject matter had no connection to my own experience. Naturally, I would draw on my senses and feelings to bring scenes alive, but the characters and situations themselves would all be purely imaginary. That freed me of the autobiographical tripwire.

In short, always be wary of 'what you know'. Whatever it is, it will benefit from additional research and the clinical gaze of the writer. Otherwise, you're writing as a reader.

What constitutes an idea for the writer?

It seems such a simple question, yet that list of misconceptions above shows how misguided many so-called ideas are. The critical thing to remember about the idea is that it is often not as big as you might initially think. It's a seed, a germ, a strand of DNA. You can't begin a novel with only an idea, because it is not yet a story, a plot, a structure. These things come later and grow organically out of the idea.

An idea can, of course, be absolutely anything. But it must be one thing above all else: something that really, *really* fascinates you. Something that keeps you awake at night with its possibilities. Something that you feel sure other people will want to hear more about. Something you find yourself chattering endlessly about or researching tirelessly on the internet. Your idea should be exactly like that rapid intake of breath, that instinctive tickling and eye-closing, just before a massive sneeze.

Your idea is the initial fuel that's going to get you through the difficulties of preparing your novel and then writing it. When you're tired, demoralised and writing with gritted teeth, it's the idea that keeps you going – this idea that you want everyone else to experience as you have. It's also the idea that eventually might sell your book.

How small can this idea be? How do you know if it meets the right criteria? How do you know it's not just a notion, a musing, a query or some other minor species of idea? We need to construct some sense of the potential that an idea represents. It could be any of these:

A theme

I'm a fan of thematic ideas. Themes can inform every element of a novel, working beneath the surface to flavour scenes, dialogue and plot points. My first book grew out of the theme of visibility and identity in Victorian London. Before photography and finger-prints, how was identity confirmed? How might a detective find a man if that man disguised himself in different clothes?

Such questions lead naturally enough into questions of perspective. Who's watching, and from where? Different perspectives provide different views, hiding and revealing, which in turn informs narrative approaches. I had no story at this stage, but the theme was one that interested me greatly.

In my fourth book, I became interested in the idea of effigy and likeness: wax models, taxidermy, prosthetics and imposters. Again, this was nowhere near a plot, but it guided everything that came after.

A story

The news is full of them. Our lives are full of them. Our culture is saturated with the concept of the story to the extent that stories structure our sense of reality. Many of them go unnoticed. An elderly man bumps into a woman on a train: the girl he met once forty years before in the Blitz. A schoolteacher absconds with his fifteen-year-old student to France. A man diving in the English Channel finds a digital camera whose photographs are retrievable. A girl walking home from school finds an ancient Greek coin on the pavement . . . any one of these could be the catalyst for a novel.

The story itself need not be the starting point of your novel. It might not even feature at all in the final version. All that's required is the germ that begins the process – the germ that fires your imagination and prompts anyone who heres it to want more.

A character

Sometimes a character is all you need. Voice and personality are such powerful things that whole books can grow out of them. We become so entranced (or appalled, or amused, or sympathetic) with a great character that we will follow them anywhere – even through a story that seems quite sparse. Martin Amis' John Self in the novel *Money* is a good example. We follow him around, listen to his thoughts, see him interact and become mesmerised by his multi-faceted unpleasantness.

A powerful character is a catalyst and a focus. He or she provides a perspective through which the reader can enter and understand the story. We see through their eyes, or we watch them through the eyes of others. The character of Captain Ahab in *Moby Dick* has entered the pantheon of great fictional characters – the epitome of obsessive self-destruction – and yet he is arguably the only real character in an otherwise huge cast. He appears relatively rarely, but is so distinctive because he is the lynchpin of the whole piece. The purpose and progress of the novel is his fatal quest.

A great character can take you anywhere. He or she generates storylines just by their presence. All you need is one, but a handful would be fantastic.

A premise

This is the eternal 'What if ... ?' question that has launched a thousand narratives – the kind of question that appeals to everyone's imagination and particularly to the marketeers who sell books.

What if Hitler had won WWII? What if the ghost of your dead father told you he'd been murdered? What if the world around us wasn't real but a computer-generated delusion? Sci-fi lives on such premises, but historical fiction can seldom resist them either. They put the reader in a position where they, too, begin to ask 'What if ... ?' and wait for the writer to confirm or deny.

I once had a job that saw me driving along a stretch of road close to which I knew the actor Nicholas Cage was filming. I wondered, 'What if he stumbled into the road and I ran him over?' It was a thought that has rattled around my head for years and this summer I wrote a comic novel based on just that premise, though neither I nor Nicholas Cage features in it.

A location

Some locations are irresistible: London, New York City, Paris, Prague. Then there are castles, gardens, streets and rooms. A place provides an anchor in space, if not in time, that can be a powerful focus for narrative. Best of all, a space naturally acquires history, contexts, characters and stories around it. It is simultaneously empty and full, static and metamorphosing. It is an idea in itself.

If a location is your idea, you'll never be short of material. The challenge is to hone and shape it so that the reader's attention moves from the general to the specific. Will the location remain the star, or will the stories and characters it suggests come to the fore? Dickens's books are not necessarily *about* London, but London is the impetus behind most of them – ever-present and supplying the dramatis personae who are both in and of the city: *sui generis*.

When you begin with a location, you're already providing extra value for your reader (and your publisher) because it's a travel book as well as a story.

A period

A man goes to a shop to buy a fish. But is it in nineteenth-century London, or seventeenth-century Madras? Is it in the ancient agora of Athens, or Berlin in 1945? Any one of these periods changes the scenario entirely and opens up a world of possibility. Historical figures can become characters. Vocabulary changes. Religions, morals and societies are different.

When you begin with a period, you remake your narrative world according to different criteria. You drop your reader into a context in which you dictate new parameters of credibility. There's a wealth of research material for you to consult and this – as we'll see – is very helpful in building your novel.

An object

I was at a loose end one day in London and decided to go down to the river near the Millennium Bridge. There's a gravel bank there that's perfect for 'mudlarking' and I like to dig around to see what a few thousand years of history have thrown up.

On that occasion, I found a few seventeenth-century clay pipe bowls, some old animal bones, some Dutch pottery fragments and a tiny glass perfume bottle. Might one of those pipes been dropped in the river during the Great Fire or the black plague? Might a ship have sunk and discarded those plates? Might a Roman lady have lost that bottle overboard on a windy day?

Objects exert a powerful influence on the imagination. A family heirloom, a meteorite, an ancient statue – they seem to have absorbed generations of human gaze or experienced journeys of ineffable wonder. They represent exactly the kind of thing that can fire your imagination and generate a novel.

A personal experience

Our own lives certainly offer a rich catalogue of occurrence. Travel, tragedy, joy and contemplation – what could be more powerful or distinctive than our first-hand experience?

But beware. Of all ideas, personal experience is most open to the risks of subjectivity. What feels compelling or fascinating or unique to us may seem banal or stereotypical to others. Travel experiences in particular tend to be broadly typical unless you've achieved some remarkable feat. Just because we associate our experiences with powerful sensations, the reader won't necessarily feel the same. Nor do our lives usually follow the rules of narrative. Events are chaotic; realisation and rationalisation come later. 'Experience' itself is only so in retrospect, once we've woven it into other contexts and narratives.

In other words, personal experience requires the same degree of artifice as any other idea if it's to become a novel. It must be treated and transformed before it will engage a reader. We can't assume that any idea from our own lives is privileged merely because it is true. Truth and fiction are like oil and water. They must form an emulsion to work.

The alternative, of course, is to write a biographical book. This has its own challenges, but gets you out of the difficulty of having to fabricate so much. The important thing is to be clear what you're doing – so many writers fall into the gap between memoir and fiction.

STOP! Don't write anything yet!

There's no reason why your idea can't include a combination of all of these things. The stronger the idea, the more potential it has. But your idea is still merely an idea, and ideas can be dangerous in this embryonic form. In their excitement to explore and develop the idea, too many writers rush into writing and discover that they run out of steam far sooner than expected. Their idea, which seemed to have such potential, turns out to be somehow less powerful in practice. This is not the idea's fault. It's still a seed; it's not yet ready to bear fruit.

Let's say you're going to start a business. You've had a brilliant idea about selling brightly coloured plates. All your friends say it's a great idea and that they'll buy one. Nobody else seems to have opened a similar shop. You'll surely make a fortune! But do you really expect the bank manager is going to hand over a loan based solely on your enthusiasm and a poll of your friends?

First, you've got to make your business plan. Where is the shop going to be? Who is going to supply you? What happens if the supply fails? How will you market your wares? Have you got insurance? There's a host of quite tedious questions that need to be asked in order to realise your brilliant idea. By the end of the process, you might feel less enthusiastic, in which case it might not work anyway.

A novel is exactly the same. Ideas are essential, but alone they are not enough. They have to be tested and shaped. Remember that many of those 99 per cent of unsuccessful submitters chose to omit this stage and sent their novel to a publisher without a business plan. The publisher saw through it in seconds. The rest of the book will explain how you turn ideas into a workable novel.

DANGER! Beware your favourite writer!

A brief word of warning. Many younger writers – those who have not yet read or written enough – tend to become fixated on their favourite writer to such an extent that they end up writing a pastiche of whoever it is. Stephenie Meyer, Terry Pratchett, George R. R. Martin and J. K. Rowling are currently some of the most copied writers in this respect. This kind of writing does not constitute an idea. At best, it's fan fiction. At worst, it's plagiarism.

Emulating your heroes is not good practice. It's a barrier to your development as a writer and a brake on your imagination. Also, you're not alone. There are tens of thousands of people doing the same thing, and none of them is going to get published because there already *is* a Stephenie Meyer, a Terry Pratchett, a George R. R. Martin. If publication is your goal, you have to create something new – a twist on your favourite genre.

A note on creative 'resilience'

At the time of writing, 'resilience' is a term much used by bodies doling out funds to public and private bodies. The claimants – a small museum, say – have to show that they have structures in place to safeguard their efforts well into the future, otherwise the money they're given will ultimately have been wasted on them.

As a professional writer, you need to be constantly having ideas. You need to be always thinking about the next book. You need to maintain your drive and enthusiasm against a tsunami of indifference. Ideas sell books. Ideas get you writing. How do you ensure a stream of ideas?

It's really nothing more than exposing yourself to influence and challenging yourself to step outside your usual frame of reference. Read widely. Visit museums and galleries. Stroll around unfamiliar streets. Talk to people you might never normally talk to: museum attendants, ticket inspectors, old women at the bus stop. Get lost among the byways of the internet. A couple of years ago, I was waiting for my wife to complete a marathon shopping odyssey in London and I wandered into the Science Museum for the first time in decades. I saw something there – an object – that intrigued me so much that I'm now researching a new novel based on it. Had I not gone into the museum, I'm sure I never would have thought of it.

And another thing about ideas: they're like rabbits. Get a few of them together and they start to generate more ideas. You might even be drawn to write non-fiction or start producing magazine articles on the unusual facts you're unearthing. If you're doing it right, you could end up with a list of future projects to look forward to. This is exactly where you need to be.

That difficult second novel

We're all familiar with the notion of the difficult second book (or album), but consider for a second why this should be the case. Admittedly, it's always tricky to follow a big success due to the weight of audience expectation, but not many first novels are that successful. The real issue tends to be that the writer has thrown years of work (and all their ideas) into their first work. When the publisher hands over the contract for the second book and you see that the deadline is just a year away, what do you do? The pot is empty.

This is not, I believe, the behaviour or attitude of a professional writer. Rather, it's the hallmark of the dilettante writer who has only ever thought of producing one book: the first book. If you want to stand any chance of building a career as a writer, you need to establish processes and behaviours whereby you're able to constantly generate workable ideas. You might even have a notebook listing them.

Perhaps, more crucially, you might find that your first published book goes down like a millstone with armbands. It happens to many writers. If your sales are low, you can guarantee you'll soon be dead to your publishers. Your name (and your brand) will be mud. What do you do then? You have no choice but to go right back to the start and write something totally different – different genre, different style, different audience. Could you do that? And could you do it *again* if the second book also fails?

It's very important to remember that your book may be a labour of love or a life statement to you, but it's nothing more than a product to the publisher, the designer and the bookseller. Your novel is one of a thousand others. If it doesn't sell, the rest will. That's why you should understand the significance of your name and your output as a brand. When the agent or the bookshop or the reader buys a book by you, what does that mean? What are they getting? When a brand becomes devalued (anyone remember Ratners?) no amount of backpedalling will win back public interest. You have to change the product and its marketing.

These are the realities of publishing. It *is* a popularity contest and you're judged on your ability to sell books. You might be the greatest stylist in the world, but if you're not hitting your sales targets, it'll be a stiffly polite email and then the echoing silence of ostracism.

So your second book should never be difficult. In fact it should be *easier* because every successive novel you write will hone your craft and your processes. You'll know you're doing it right because your average daily word count will increase, the time taken to complete the novel will decrease and you'll actually be excited about the next book, and the next. Ideas will flock about you like pigeons in Trafalgar Square.

> *For a true writer each book should be a new beginning where he tries again for something that is beyond attainment. He should always try for something that has never been done or that others have tried and failed. Then sometimes, with great luck, he will succeed.*
>
> Ernest Hemingway (cited in Baker, 1992)

The idea in summary

- It's the idea that sells the book – not the writing.
- The idea is the start of the process, not the end.
- The author's initial idea may not be the publisher's marketing idea.
- 'What you know' is not enough.
- Be open-minded about where ideas come from.
- Emulation is not an idea.
- You need to be always having ideas.

Idea-building exercises

- Scan through today's newspaper for one story you think could become a novel idea. What might you add? What might you change?

- Choose three of your favourite novels and attempt to summarise the essential idea (not necessarily the story) of the book in a single sentence, making it sound as appealing as possible to someone who's not read it.
- Choose three of the idea criteria listed in this chapter (theme, character, location, period, etc.) and apply them to the story you pulled out of the newspaper. How might you flesh out that idea and make it your own?
- Start a fresh new notebook in which you jot ideas for future novels. It doesn't matter how vague at this point, just as long as you're always thinking.
- Practise writing the back-cover blurb for the novel you're planning or working on. It's quite difficult, but it helps you to focus on the essential idea.
- Go to a museum or gallery and find an exhibit that suggests an idea to you. What would be the next step in terms of research?
- Make a list of recent bestsellers and try to summarise the essential idea behind each title. Why do you think they were published?
- Practise 'pitching' your idea to friends or a reading group and see what questions they ask. These questions will help you add dimension to your idea.

3   Building story

An idea may initially be a fragmentary tale or a premise, but it's usually not enough to generate 70,000-plus coherent words. The idea has potential but is essentially finite. 'What if . . . ?' is a great question, but it's the fabric of the answer we need.

Texture is critical. Many first novels fail because they are too sparse, too threadbare. They are lacking in incident, in character, in theme, in story – overall, in *depth* and *texture*. This is caused largely by insufficient time spent building the story elements.

By story, we don't necessarily mean plot (to be discussed in the next chapter). Nor do we mean only a basic sequence of occurrences. What's needed at this developmental stage is the vast accumulation of detail that will be used to construct a workable plan for the novel. It means teasing, stretching and expanding your original idea into a web of narrative possibility.

It is a highly creative and enjoyable experience, but it is criminally neglected on many courses and in many books about writing. There's an assumption that the process should somehow be instinctive for genuine writers, though the truth is that many first-time novelists seem unaware of this highly important stage. It's something that people believe 'will just come' when they start writing. When it doesn't, they are nonplussed. So let's be clear:

Story building is not the same as writing.

Yes – the actual process of writing does implicitly suggest and inform story elements. Writing without aim can sometimes generate further ideas. We're not talking about that. We're talking about an entirely different – quite separate – skill that every serious writer should learn. It has nothing to do with showing and telling, dialogue or punctuation. It has everything to do with the elements of a novel that make it memorable for the reader, that engage a reader and give the book personality, depth, texture.

Think back through some of your favourite books. What's the first thing you remember – the first and most powerful recollection? Is it the sentence on page 114 where he uses that deft dash to show hesitation? Is it the clever bit on page 243 where she uses the series of staccato one-line paragraphs to pick up the pace? I'd be astounded if it was. Fine writing undoubtedly enhances our enjoyment of a good book, but it's not what we remember. Nor – paradoxically enough – is the entire plot, which is too lengthy to recall in a moment. In building story, we need to begin with the elements that readers enjoy and remember.

Some things we remember in books

- Enthralling/hilarious/shocking episodes
- Amazing twists and revelations
- Distinctive characters and their voices
- Themes and ideas that made us think
- A sense of place – of being there
- A state of mind or altered perception
- How we felt while reading the book
- The overall trick the author pulled off.

I'm sure you have your own examples. Some of mine are: the bit in *Lolita* when she sits on Humbert's lap; Queequeg in his coffin in *Moby Dick*; the gradual slide into the fabulous in Umberto Eco's *Baudolino*; the Hollywood offspring forming their own subculture of failure in Joyce Carol Oates' *Blonde*. These were things that grew out of the authors' original ideas: the progeny of those ideas. So how do we build story out of an idea?

Research

For some reason, research is often overlooked by many first-time novelists. Maybe it's because there's so little time to actually write that people would rather spend the time at a keyboard. The urge to write is good, but it's a false economy in the end because it prevents you from learning an equally necessary skill.

Other writers don't consider research because they believe they already know everything they need to know. Either that, or they believe that imagination and the writing process itself will conjure all the necessary detail. Indeed, many established authors are disingenuous about how much research they actually do. Surely research is a sign of a weak imagination!

It's interesting, however, if you compare novel-writing with almost any other form of professional writing. A journalist wouldn't think of writing a long feature on a famous person without first getting deep into research. At the very least, there'd be an interview and a glance at what the star had said in previous notable interviews. A commercial copywriter wouldn't dream of writing a report or a proposal or a strategy without a huge amount of fact-gathering and investigation into objectives, budgets and audience type. A screenwriter working on a film might spend more time researching the project than it actually takes to write the thing.

The reason why such writers do research is blindingly simple. When you have a glut of information to hand, the writing becomes easier. You're free to pick the best bits from it, find patterns in it and trace stories through it. Your germ of an idea begins to flourish and take on many more dimensions of possibility. It might even become an entirely different idea. The research I did for my first novel gave me plot ideas and characters for four more books.

The aim of research is first to accumulate a glut of fertile information around your idea. It will form the raw material of your novel, from which you will then pull plot strands, themes, characters and scenes in order to structure the novel.

It can be a lengthy and highly involved process, but you need to be patient. This is a necessary part of the novel-writing process and will arm you with the tools to become an all-round professional. Naturally, research for a historical novel might take months or years, whereas research for a novel about your hometown might take a fortnight. Why do any research at all for the latter? Because I guarantee you'll find something you hadn't known.

Below, I'll provide a case study of how research for one of my own books produced the necessary materials to build the story. But first, a brief question.

Where do you do your research?

It's really too broad a question to cover properly here. The short version is that the internet has made things immeasurably easier than they used be. There are databases, archives, online libraries and endless chat rooms where you can instantly learn what you need. Different projects will require different sources. A few of the most obvious places to go are:

Your public library

If they haven't got the book you want, they can almost always get it from a library elsewhere in the UK (for a small fee). Don't underestimate the power of the entire British Library at your disposal.

Online booksellers

I'm not being facetious. You might think that just because a book is out of print or two hundred years old you're never going to find a copy. Wrong. Many antiquarian booksellers work through Amazon. I bought a six-volume encyclopaedia of London (printed in 1844) from one of them and it's been invaluable.

Online archives

The Times Digital Archive, for example, has every copy of *The Times* from the eighteenth century into the late twentieth century. You can view it online for free with a public library card, along with many other historical newspaper archives. I got four books out of it.

Museums and galleries

It sounds obvious but seeing history as physical objects is far more compelling than just reading about them or seeing pictures.

Personal interviews

Ask any journalist and they'll tell you how endlessly surprising interviews can be. You think you know what the subject is going to say, and they lead you off into a whole other story you'd never considered. People are the best sources of stories.

Physical research

Go there. I downloaded a free 1847 map of London and took it with me on a fact-finding mission in the capital. It turned out to be one of the most fascinating experiences of my life, following vanished roads and correlating the things I'd made up with the real buildings of my research. In one place, I was able to note a peculiar detail of an actual street and use it as a twist in my big ending. We see differently when we're researching. We look more closely.

A word on sources

If you begin with secondary sources, you'll soon see that most writers are using the same pool of primary sources. So should you. When you deal with primary sources, there can be no accusation of error or fabrication. No matter how bizarre or incredible your facts are, you'll know they're genuine.

By limiting yourself to primary sources, you also increase your chances of turning up material that nobody else has used. I've discovered stories in nineteenth-century newspapers that formed major plot elements in my books.

What do you look for?

The nature of your idea will dictate the main thrust of your research directions, but you should keep your eye out for all the things you'd never considered: the little facts and details, the digressions, the local colour that lends veracity and engagement to your stories and characters. So many books are memorable for the little things that turn out to be entirely extraneous to the plot: James Bond's favourite jam, the bologna sandwiches in *The Shipping News*, the chowder in *Moby Dick*, the description of saddle harnesses in Cormac McCarthy's books.

As you pursue the natural trails of your research, keep an eye out for such things as:

- Potential story threads
- Interesting/esoteric/arcane vocabulary
- Product names (brands help pinpoint a period or culture)
- Processes and practices
- Character types
- Food – always representative of something
- Sensory evocations (smells and sounds bring description to life)
- Additional ideas and related stories
- Expansions on theme.

> *Making people believe the unbelievable is no trick; it's work. . . . Belief and reader absorption come in the details: an overturned tricycle in the gutter of an abandoned neighbourhood can stand for everything.*
>
> Stephen King (2012)

Should you read similar novels as research?

Some do; some don't. I have an aversion to it because my own approach involves absorbing a load of stuff quite arbitrarily and picking the best bits out of it. With such a method, I'm afraid I might inadvertently steal someone else's details or (worse) fragments of their plot. Consequently, I avoided reading any Victorian crime novels while writing my own. I read only one of Dickens's (*Oliver Twist*) before realising that his London was altogether too close to the one I wanted to create. My book had to come purely from primary research and imagination.

Other – less paranoid – writers might benefit from finding out what's already been written in order to do something different. There is one potential pitfall to this, though. My experience is that many first-time novelists with an interest in a particular genre do occasionally tend to produce pastiches of their favourite authors. It's usually unconscious – a symptom of absorbing too much of one writer or genre at the expense of some wider reading.

It's also worth remembering that any detail you pick up from novels is potentially a tertiary source. As a writer yourself, you will realise that fiction is just another way of telling lies. You're supposed to believe what you read in a novel, but that doesn't mean it was ever true. Use novels for ideas and inspiration, certainly, but beware of taking them at face value.

How do you know you've done enough?

Without a specific plot or structure in mind, you might feel you don't have any clear indicators of when you've done enough research. The first case study below will provide the clearest guidance on this question, but you'll also find, after some time, that you begin to turn up the same kind of information across all of your sources.

The simplest indicator is that you reach a kind of critical mass: you have so many ideas, so much input, such a wealth of material that you know you're ready to start working with it. Certain facts will begin to reoccur. You might feel like this after a week, or after six months. It depends on the kind of book you're writing.

At the same time, it's important that you realise something most first-time novelists do not:

There's more content in a novel than you realise.

By content, I mean characters, storylines, locations, themes and the overall texture. Many novels have a number of concurrent and interwoven storylines. They have a cast of primary, secondary and incidental characters. They have twenty or thirty or fifty chapters. This is a lot of content, which has to come from somewhere. Imagination supplies a lot, but raw materials are more than useful.

As an example, here's a very basic breakdown o
novel *The Vice Society*. Apart from the major char
vague idea for the book, I had none of this detail until t
was completed:

Components of a commercial novel

- 28 chapters of about 3,000 words each
- 6 major (series) characters
- 9 secondary characters
- 11 incidental characters
- 22 locations
- Three interwoven storylines
- An entire historical period
- Interest areas: pornographic books, prostitution, private clubs.

That was a historical novel. There's no reason why a novel can't work with just two characters and one location, but such a novel would attain its texture by other means. Not by detail, necessarily, but by occurrence. Things would have to be always happening in order to keep the reader's attention. Or the narrator's voice would have to be so compelling that the reader would be willing to follow him even if nothing much was happening. Both of these options are quite challenging in a first novel.

Let's consider my two favourite literary novels. *Lolita* is pretty much a two-character piece, and even Lolita has very little to say for herself. The texture is supplied by Humbert's mesmeric voice, by Nabokov's scintillating style, by the structure (see also Chapter 4, 'Construction') and by various narrative movements that direct the reader's attention. It's less 'busy' than commercial fiction and less happens, but it arguably has more depth.

In *Moby Dick*, the cast is huge and the principal location is the ship – ideal for the purposes of allegory. The story of Ahab's search for the white whale runs alongside an encyclopaedia of whale lore and observations of the crew. Occurrence and straightforward information-giving keep the novel moving along and much of the action is peripheral to the quest for the whale – essentially side-narratives. The book is everything Herman Melville knew about whaling and about life spread over a very loose narrative thread – another journey.

Again, are the textural components of a literary novel radically different from those of a commercial novel? There may be fewer of them, but their depth and complexity might be greater. The aim is the same: to keep the reader engaged with a multiplicity of levels. Any major differences are likely to be in terms of style and structure, since all novels must contain characters, locations, storylines and subject areas.

Chapter 4 (Construction) considers these matters in more depth, but it's worth thinking at this stage what kind of novel you think yours might be. This in turn will inform what you need to gather.

Some novel approaches

- A voice-led novel (relatively few active characters but a powerful protagonist)
- A character-led novel ('chick lit', for example)
- A novel of occurrence (crime and thriller, for example)
- A historical novel (lots of detail)
- A literary novel (ripe with themes and style)
- A pseudo-memoir (a convincing chronology and associated characters).

Alternatively, you might not have any idea what kind of novel you want to write, and that's not at all a bad thing. Better to feel out your project than rush into it with an idea but no resources. The following case studies show some examples of how an original idea moves into research and then into the story-building process.

Different novels, different requirements

Different books will of course have different processes. Below, we'll look at a couple of case studies taken from my own books and also take a stab at *Lolita*, so to speak. *The Vice Society*, for example, was a historical novel and so required a considerable amount of research. Also, it grew out of a thematic idea, which tends to be a loose concept rather than a firm narrative tool. If

Table 3.1 Idea research approaches

Original idea	Research	Story-building map
A character or characters	Their locations, job details, dress, language, backstories, friends	Their inter-relationships, motivations, conflicts and individual storylines
A location	Its history, fabric, people, places, reputation, sounds	Episodes, themes, narrative patterns, characters, conflicts, contrasts
An object	Its history and provenance, its path of ownership, its manufacture, its significance, others like it, the characters around it	Timelines, episodes, patterns, themes, related locations, path of ownership
A 'What if . . . ?' premise	(Depends on the premise)	Possibilities of occurrence and influence, characters drawn in, episodes generated, follow-on storylines, unexpected discoveries
A voice	(Depends on the voice)	A challenge, trajectory or narrative journey – characters to meet, relationships with them. Conflicts, obstacles, episodes, opportunities

your starting point is a character or a location, your research and story-building process is likely to be different. If you begin with a location, a period and a character, your research will be far more focused. In different cases, you might spend far more time on the mapping than on collecting detail, or vice versa.

Table 3.1 on the previous page shows a very generic imagining of how different approaches might affect your research and story-building. (It's clearly not possible to be exhaustive because there's no limit to the variations.)

Story-building case studies

The first two case studies below concentrate on the preparatory work done before a word is written. I think it's the easiest and most streamlined way to produce a book. It's also true that for some writers these story-building techniques may (and will) grow out of the actual writing process itself, but this tends to come with experience. Attempting to build story 'on the hop' in a first novel very often ends in a situation like the kitchen disaster when you get to the end of making a meal and realise you forgot to do the fried onions first (or add the tinned tomatoes). You've made something, but you might not want to eat it. The most important thing to remember is that story-building is something you need to think carefully about.

Story-Building Case Study 1

The Vice Society (Pan Macmillan, 2010)

1 The idea

My first book, *The Incendiary's Trail* (Pan Macmillan, 2009), had established a suite of characters I planned to use in an ongoing Victorian crime series. When a second book was commissioned, I was therefore in a good position as regards characters and general location. I didn't have a story or a plot, but I did have an idea that had been suggested by research for the first book.

Reading *The Times*, I'd come across a few stories about suicides from the Monument. These were related in such a grisly and yet heartbreaking manner that I felt compelled to visit the Monument itself. I became certain that such a suicide would make a gripping first chapter. But who could I kill? Why not make it the wife of my detective, Mr Williamson? This would be a great catalyst for a story and a compelling reason for him to investigate, especially if it hadn't been a suicide at all.

This, then, was my idea. It was not enough for a plot, but it was a start. Now I could begin my research.

2 The research

It seems to me that there are two broad ways into research. The most conventional and probably the simplest is to have a good idea what you're looking for and to pursue it in all the right places. But sometimes you're not sure what you're looking for – only the places where it might be found. In this case, you just have to immerse yourself in the subject area and dig around until you hit a vein of gold. I favour the second method. It seems to offer more possibilities by suggesting things I'd never considered.

I began by reading all (primary source) eye-witness accounts of suicides from the Monument. This didn't take long. Thereafter, I followed my usual approach of reading randomly whatever caught my attention within the period. Newspapers are great for this, presenting a variety of stories that act as threads to follow in more detailed books. If I read about a housewife being killed by prussic acid, I'd go off and research prussic acid. If I saw an advert for 'Thompson's Bowel Gravel Alleviation Pills', I might look into bowel gravel (so to speak). You never know what might make a good story.

In fact, my research for *The Vice Society* turned up an unsolved death of 1849 that became a critical plot point in

(continued)

(continued)

the book. It was a brief story, appearing in *The Times* over a few days, in which the inexplicable nature of the death and the evasiveness of all witnesses suggested a much deeper mystery. The real case fizzled out for lack of evidence, but I was happy to take it up.

Throughout the research period, I made notes in small notebooks: interesting details, statistics, quotes, processes and products. I had no grand design – just accumulating things that seemed fascinating to me and which I hoped readers might like to hear about.

3 The REALLY IMPORTANT bit

But I wasn't just collecting things willy-nilly. That could have gone on for years. As well as my small notebooks, I kept a different book in which I began to collect something far more important than interesting historical nuggets. It was divided into these categories:

- Themes
- Characters
- Episodes
- Storylines
- Locations
- Words.

As I researched, I jotted any further ideas under these headings. Everything was provisional. Everything was merely a suggestion. I might end up with twenty new minor and major characters sourced from my reading. I might think of thirty exciting or unusual episodes I could use. The Monument was my first location, but how many others would provide memorable scenes? And as I gathered these things, I was also asking the 'What if . . . ?' question to see what possible storylines might connect these disparate parts. (The 'words' category was purely a vocabulary thing – I like to throw in a few arcane period words for local colour.)

At this stage, I still wasn't thinking about an overarching plot. That would materialise by itself as the constructive elements of the book moved closer towards each other. After a few months, the fleshed-out categories probably looked something like this (only with many more entries over numerous pages):

Table 3.2 Story-building elements for *The Vice Society* (1)

Themes	Characters	Episodes
Immorality	Street urchin	Snowstorm
Guilt	Prostitute	Suicide
Sin	Spoilt heir	Autism quiz
Salvation	Bookseller	Interrogation
Revenge	Spy	Accident (?)
Trust	Courtesan	Spanking den
	Scullery maid	Slaughterhouse
	Insane guy	
	Landlady	
	Fall victim	
	Dissolute lord	
	Doctor	

By this stage, I still hadn't written a word of the novel, whose working title was *The Persephone Letter*. The materials I had to work with were:

- A set of core characters
- A primary location (London)

(continued)

(continued)

Table 3.3 Story-building elements for *The Vice Society* (2)

Storylines	Locations	Words
Blackmail plot	Smithfield	Algolagnia
Mail fraud	Temple Bar	Depucelate
Porn selling	Clerkenwell	Klismophilia
Kidnap	Wapping	Fustigate
Rescue	Opium den	
The vice club	Private club	
Conspiracy	Library	
Murder × 2	Scotland Yard	
The letter	Holywell St.	
Poisoned girls	Bookshop	
	Haymarket	

- A cast of new characters
- A clutch of possible episodes and locations
- Some disconnected possible storylines
- A sense of the kind of novel I wanted to write (see below)
- A projected word count of about 90,000–100,000 words.

My original idea was slowly accruing a greater density, but I needed a stronger idea of how all these elements might combine into a more coherent structure. If we look again at the tables, it seems tantalisingly to suggest numerous connections even in its tabulated form. Is there enough material to begin plotting? The next stage of the process tests where gaps might exist.

4 Mapping the material

Lists and columns are not particularly conducive to creative connections. There's also so much material that it's ever more likely to become confused or frustrated. Too much information, after all, can be as bad as not enough.

One way to reassess what you have is to create a spider diagram featuring the major elements of your research material – your characters, your locations, your episodes, etc. – and to start drawing connecting lines between them. How might they relate? How might they suggest story threads? As you do this, questions will naturally start to arise. The exercise invites you to ask 'What if . . . ?'

The diagram for *The Vice Society* looked something like this (only with much more detail):

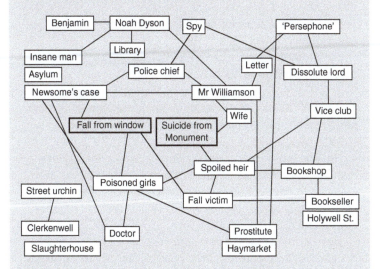

Figure 3.1 Story-building elements for *The Vice Society*

Seeing it all laid out thus, the questions begin to arise:

What if XX visited the asylum?
What if YY received a letter from PP?

(continued)

(continued)

What if DD heard a rumour about the blackmail?
What if the spy was forced to spy on XX?
What if the snowstorm coincided with the slaughterhouse scene?

Such questions then lead on to others:

Where is XX when we first meet him?
Why would YY visit that place anyway?
How would XX know he was being spied on?
How can I connect XX and PP?
Why does PP care about YY?
How does RR know XX?

This is still NOT a plot, however. A plot has a number of other requirements that will be addressed in the next chapter. This is a clutch of potential story elements that you'll use to construct a plot. The more story elements you have, and the higher the number of possible connections, the easier your plot will eventually be to create. As story elements multiply, they begin to reach towards each other as tentacles until a single organism begins to form.

Even in this simplified form, the material is starting to show persuasive links and narrative possibilities. Some episodes seem irresistibly to offer themselves; others seem isolated and may need reassessing. The shaded boxes, for example, seem to suggest two attention-grabbing scenes that might act as catalysts for the action, though there might be a dozen different plots in this loose matrix.

As you go on interrogating your material, you'll start to see where you need another character, a bridging scene, a justification for someone or an extra episode. Storylines will begin to grow closer, suggesting parallels and possible new directions. The material will begin to reach critical mass as you get a sense you're near the stage when you have enough to attempt a plot. You might even begin to discard certain elements as extraneous (and keep them for future books).

What's most important is creating enough stuff here for a novel of texture and occurrence. With such a diagram in hand, I might go back to the research to clarify a few extra points or source another character with whom to make a connection. The entire process is one that could take weeks or months, but this is valuable thinking time that will result in a detailed plan. It's exactly the kind of thinking that many writers don't do, instead launching into a book that ends up thin and meandering due to lack of content.

In the case of *The Vice Society*, the elements of story started to come together quite quickly once I got to the mapping stage. Starting with those two deaths, I assigned one to each of my two detectives (Williamson and Newsome) as the stimuli for their investigations. I had no idea why the deaths had occurred or how they might eventually connect, which led me to posit a reason common to both (the villain) and to work backwards to fill the gaps. That decision naturally involved further mapping and character creation.

It can be a messy and sometimes frustrating process, but it's also very exciting. Few things are more creative than forging a story (or multiple stories) from a mass of detail. Anything is possible. You can put your characters in any location and drop them into the most challenging situations to see how they get out. If something doesn't work on paper, you simply rub it out and rethink (rather than having to redraft 20,000 words later.)

Story-Building Case Study 2

Holiday Nightmare **(currently unpublished, 2012)**

This case study was something quite different from *The Vice Society*. *Holiday Nightmare* was a novel based very strongly on personal experience and so I already had much of the knowledge I needed. However, this was a book I'd been unable to write for years because I was so hung up on the biographical element. Only when I decided to make my experience a small strand of a larger imaginary narrative, and to research new possibilities, did it become possible. This was the book I wrote in ten weeks.

1 The idea

I once worked as a resort rep on a Greek island where a Hollywood film was being made. The experiences I had during the job seemed made for a novel, while the glamour of the movie-making business seemed to add another dimension. I idly wondered one day what might happen if I ran over the star of the film: Nicholas Cage . . .

2 The research

I didn't have to research the island or the job. As well as many powerful memories of the place, I also had a journal from the time that contained numerous characters and scenarios I could use. The problem, however, was that my experiences in themselves formed only a weak narrative for a single-perspective story. There wasn't enough. I'd have to flesh out the truth with a lot more fiction.

So, even though I'd lived in Greece for three years, I started some research. My initial reading suggested a few other characters that interested me: a policeman, a priest, a movie star, an archaeology professor, an ultra-nationalist and a production assistant. I knew very little about any of these people or their jobs. What did they wear? What was the vocabulary specific to their lives? How might they speak and what would be their preoccupations? This was my next bit of research.

In contrast to my historical novels, which typically took four or six months to research, this one took about three weeks. I read a few books on movie-making, a few actors' biographies and the rest was easily found on the internet. Critically, this three weeks' work gave me enough material to start building a story I knew could lend texture to a novel.

3 The REALLY IMPORTANT bit

As with *The Vice Society*, I kept informal lists to help direct my story-building. The information for *Holiday Nightmare* probably looked something like this:

Table 3.4 Story-building elements for *Holiday Nightmare* (1)

Themes	Characters	Episodes
Real/fake	Rep	Quiz night
Greece v. 'Greece'	PA	Accident
Faith/belief	Star	Complaints
Experience	Policeman	The discovery
Retribution	Priest	Kidnap
	Nationalist	Filming
	Professor	Pagan rites
		Earthquake

4 Mapping the material

This book was considerably easier to map because some of the storylines already existed. The challenge was to see how

(continued)

(continued)

Table 3.5 Story-building elements for *Holiday Nightmare* (2)

Storylines	Locations
Film rewrites	The set
Rep problems	Police office
Priest crusade	Ancient site
Romances	The beach
Missing star	The village
Keeping job	The bar
Investigation	The airport
	Homes
	The church

they might combine and complement each other rather than exist as separate strands. The mapping process looked something like Figure 3.2 on the opposite page.

Again, relationships, storylines and scenes are already suggesting themselves. Questions begin to arise:

How does the nationalist get connected to the church?
How does the rep meet the PA?
How does the priest discover the pagan rites?
How does the star get kidnapped and why?
Does the professor know the rep?
Where do all these people live?

Whereas *The Vice Society* mapping appeared to suggest a novel that might begin with two notable occurrences, this one appears to have a group of characters at its centre. Such deductions are helpful, but also potentially misleading at this early stage.

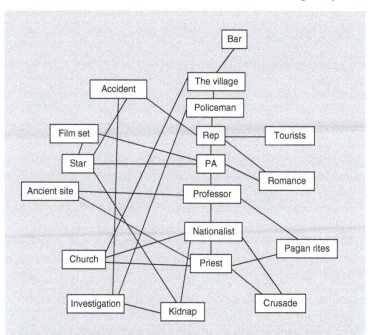

Figure 3.2 Story-building elements for *Holiday Nightmare*

Again, we're NOT yet considering plot at this stage of the process – just trying to find a way into the novel. It would be too easy to rush into writing, only to realise later that the storylines don't match up, that the episodes are unconnected, or that a character doesn't seem to be working – all the kinds of things listed above.

The story-building stage is about gathering your materials so that you begin the novel with an abundant resource. In the case of *Holiday Nightmare*, I ended up deciding on eight separate storylines, each one connected to a major character. How those eight storylines managed to work together would be a matter of plotting and construction.

Story-Building Case Study 3 *(Spoiler alert!)*

Lolita by **Vladimir Nabokov (1955)**

Naturally, I can have no possibility of knowing how Nabokov wrote his masterpiece or how he accumulated his research. This is usually true for any book we read as a reader. However, it might be an interesting and instructive exercise to speculate, in reverse, how a book might have achieved its final form. This teaches us to read more critically as writers and to look for the hidden mechanisms. The following will, then, be a work of speculative fiction applied retroactively to *Lolita*. It's probably not how Nabokov wrote it, but it's how we might approach a first novel.

1 The idea

A letter sent by Nabokov during the gestation period of *Lolita* mentioned that he was writing a book called *The Kingdom by the Sea* about a man who likes little girls. Uncoincidentally, there's an Edgar Allan Poe poem called *Annabel Lee* (the name of Humbert's first love in *Lolita*), which features the repeated phrase 'the kingdom by the sea'. Academics have since found plentiful evidence of *Lolita*'s origins in Nabokov's life and work, but here is a germ of an idea. From this – the very origin of the novel – he builds the larger story of Humbert's liaison with Lolita.

2 The research

Much of the book's local colour is based on Nabokov's own peregrinations about the country in his hunt for butterfly specimens (he was a noted lepidopterist) and so the detailed descriptions of road trips and motels are undoubtedly drawn from experience. In understanding the world of Lolita herself, though, the author clearly spent some time looking at teen magazines, teen fashions and teen music – things that were presumably outside his typical areas of interest. He must also have done some research into the legal definitions and discussions around pederasty, because we find a number of facts pointing to its dubious legitimacy in certain parts of the world or in literature.

3 The REALLY IMPORTANT bit

Having decided on his idea, Nabokov would have known automatically what other elements were required: a backstory for his protagonist Humbert (explaining his predelictions); a location for the story to begin playing out; secondary characters necessary as storyline agents; locations to act as stepping stones on the road trip; some essential steps in the story from meeting Lolita to becoming her illicit lover; and thematic discussions to be had along the way. There would also have been an overarching aim for what the novel was to achieve as a piece of satirical work and as a game with the form of the novel itself. These are the basic ingredients he must have gathered.

4 Mapping the material

This was not Nabokov's first novel. Plus, he was one of the greatest novelists ever. It seems unlikely he mapped his material for *Lolita* as we might map a first novel. He knew instinctively how to plan a story and could have written it in whatever order he liked. Still, it might be interesting to imagine a diagram (Figure 3.3, below) just to see what options present themselves at this early stage.

A number of structural elements become immediately apparent just from the arrangement of characters and locations. There's a two-level backstory (Annabel Lee and Humbert's first

(continued)

(continued)

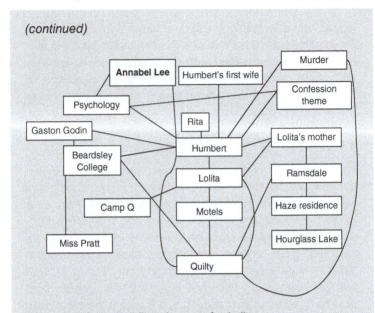

Figure 3.3 Story-building elements for *Lolita*

wife) and indeed the whole thing is told in retrospect as a prison-cell confession. There's a section in which Nabokov arrives in Ramsdale and meets Lolita. There's the road trip and its pause at Beardsley College. The characters necessary for each transition are all in place: Lolita's mother as the landlady in Ramsdale; Gaston Godin as the man Humbert knows at Beardsley; Rita as the woman who accompanies Humbert during a different, quite discrete, period. Note how Quilty – the man who will take Lolita – seems to be connected at almost every level. The characters and locations group automatically together. You can see the novel urging itself into different sections.

A note on story

Story is often misunderstood as simply 'what happens' in the book. It's very seldom a single thread. Rather, it's multiple threads (theme, character, occurrence) developing together throughout the novel. As you start to build your story, you should consider a range of other, associated, matters such as:

- What is the possible trajectory of each individual character? Where do they start, where do they go, how do they get there, how do they meet, what do they learn, what do they want and where do they end up? How does interaction with other characters affect this trajectory? Can you identify a number of key events in your characters' story?

- How will you move characters between locations? What motivation do they have to move around? For example, Nabokov introduces the character of Gaston Godin as a reason for Humbert and Lolita to go to Beardsley College.

- How might you explore your chosen themes in terms of storyline, episode and character? Can you map a thematic arc? I once read a book whose loose structure was arranged around the Kübler-Ross model of grieving a loved one: denial, anger, bargaining, depression and acceptance.

- If you already know some of the key events in your story, where might these fall in the book? Do you need them to be right at the beginning, or can they happen later? Do they have to feature at all (they might be alluded to as part of a backstory)?

- Story is the thing the reader will work with – the thing that keeps them interested in reading on. A story asks the reader to recognise, question, predict, expect, infer and eventually be satisfied with the various things happening in the novel. What have you got to offer your reader in these terms?

- A story doesn't move only from beginning to end. The reader is always looking back and mentally referencing what they've already read. Writing as a writer, you need to ensure that your story works backwards and forwards. For example, you need only include a backstory element if it's necessary to the understanding of a character or an on-going storyline. If the reader doesn't need to reference that backstory at any later stage, it may be irrelevant. Or when a character appears apparently out of the blue, the reader will remember two previous chapters where that person was lurking in the shadows, thus completing a narrative circuit.

- NOTE: it's not necessary at this stage for you to know the full extent of your story (though it would be very handy). What's important is that you have sufficient pieces to start dropping into a structural framework. The various requirements of plot and structure will help you to develop more parts of the story.

Story-building in summary

- An idea needs texture to become a novel.
- Story-building is a process independent from writing.
- Texture makes books memorable (and readable) – not writing alone.
- Research aids imagination.
- Be structured in your accumulation and recording of detail.
- Map your research to interrogate the possibilities.
- Consider what kind of story yours might be (quest, biographical, etc.).
- Work on storylines until you feel you have enough for plotting.
- Don't worry if you haven't got the entire story. Plotting will help.

Story-building exercises

- Outline areas you might research to flesh out your idea. Keep a notebook of potential characters, locations, themes, storylines and episodes you might like to write.
- Draw a spider diagram of your idea as it develops, including characters, locations, themes and storylines. What connections can you find between them? What questions arise? Can you see any patterns (or gaps) emerging?
- Begin to think about possible storylines and write them down for future reference. How do storylines start? How many steps/stages are there in each story? How might they intertwine with other storylines?

- Make brief character notes. You needn't necessarily think about backstory, but do consider what motivates your characters. What do they want? Will they get it? This will help you with storylines.
- As well as major characters (those with their own story), consider secondary or tertiary agents of plot: people who need to appear to reveal, explain or symbolise something.
- Give some thought to possible major events or movements in your novel. These can act as milestones when you start to think about structure.
- If your notes seem disconnected – just a jumble of pieces – go back to your research. An additional character, theme or storyline might be the connecting device you need.
- Try talking out some of your storylines with a friend. You'll find that the mental process of trying to put it all in order will help you to fill gaps. Also, people tend to ask questions you might not have considered.

4   Construction

Construction is difficult. It's the most difficult and possibly the least pleasurable aspect of writing a novel – a discipline that even established authors find difficult or which they actively avoid for just this reason.

The difficulty, I think, stems partly from the perception that novel construction is so utterly alien to the creative power of writing. It's a mechanical and highly calculated activity that seems to offer only 'rules' and to stifle the free flow of imagination with rigid guidelines. The common aversion to it goes back to that fallacy that writing is the panacea for everything – that simply writing will automatically generate the answers to everything.

But let's consider other art forms for a moment. When Renaissance painters were experimenting with perspective, composition, pigments and different forms of application, were they somehow wasting good painting time? When a composer lays out the score for his symphony using movements and classical structures, is he just avoiding the instruments? When a sculptor makes numerous sketches or maquettes, is it because he's reluctant to pick up the hammer and chisel?

Preparation is integral to the artistic process. Selection and rejection are critical to creating the finished article. When you see the perfect photograph, you don't see the 200 others that didn't get chosen. When the reader reads your book, they don't see the scribbled plot notes or the character you cut or the editor's amendments or the punctuation errors the copy-editor took out. As writers, we have to go through all of this. We want to conceive our novel as a perfect form, but we have to go through the frustration of seeing it ragged, patchy, fragmentary and flawed.

It helps to conceive the construction phase in a clinical manner. Like a doctor attending to a seriously ill patient, you have to cool-headedly assess symptoms, apply diagnostic tools and plan a treatment that's in the best interest of the patient. You can't be distracted by the haemorrhaging or the screaming. Stick to your professional skills and you have the best chance of effecting a complete recovery.

Constructing a novel requires many different considerations. This chapter will address most of them in as intuitive an order as possible. Nevertheless, the truth is that construction is rarely an ordered process. All of these considerations coalesce at different times and at different speeds. Only by considering them all can you hope to get your novel into a workable shape. My recommendation is that you do so before you write a word, but the approach remains just as relevant for a final draft (with the downside that you'll have to do a huge amount of rewriting).

> *It's none of their business that you have to learn to write. Let them think you were born that way.*
> Ernest Hemingway (cited in Gabriel, 2014)

Story, plot, narrative, structure

What's the difference? It depends who you ask. The academic world could offer thousands of words on each one, but that's not much help to you. For the purposes of this chapter, let's settle on these working definitions.

Story is a summary of what happens in the novel. There may be just one, or a number of them intertwined as storylines. There may be stories within the storylines. Some can be related quite simply. Joseph Conrad's *Heart of Darkness*, for example, is about a career sailor called Marlow sailing up the Congo to discover a man named Kurtz, who has gone insane. Of course there are many more incidents along the way, but this is the broad sweep of it. (And then there's the question of what it's *really* about, which we'll come to later.) In *Lolita*, a man named Humbert Humbert absconds with an underage girl whose mother has fortuitously died. Again, there are numerous episodes within this basic story. Thrillers typically contain far more complicated stories because this keeps the reader's attention. Literature typically relies more on voice and style (with the result that not an awful lot seems to happen in some very long books). It's important to note that the order in which we summarise the story is not necessarily the order in which it is told in a plot.

The plot is the pattern on which the stories are laid out or *told*. Plot uses mechanisms to separate, stagger, withhold and order the occurrences of story. There are introductions, developments, cliffhangers, twists and dénouements. A plot might be linear or move around in time, In fact, both *Lolita* and *Heart of Darkness* have periods of looking back. In the former, we look back from the notional present to the period of the story and to a time before that for context. In the latter, almost the entire story is told in retrospect.

Genre books are typically strong on plot and pull the reader through with a 'page-turning' impulse. Literary novels are often said not to have plots at all in the sense of compelling structures, though it depends on your viewpoint whether this is a good or a bad thing. 'Plotless' novels appear to develop organically, relying on style or voice to carry the day. Henry Miller's *Tropic of Cancer* arguably has neither plot nor story and can be a challenging read for just this reason, but it's nevertheless a great evocation of a writer finding his voice. Céline's *Journey to the End of the Night* is essentially a chronological series of very loosely connected sections whose cohesion lies in the narrator's voice. I'd argue that every book requires some kind of plot, otherwise why would the reader want to read to the end? The plot gives shape to a novel.

Narrative is how the plot relates story. It makes choices about perspective, tense, occurrence and character voice – the actual relating of the story as text. Narrative is what absorbs the reader into the action. More than these other constructive categories, it represents the creative aspect of the writing. Let's say our story offers us a young sailor as the protagonist. The plot dictates that we meet him in Chapter 2 and the narrative decides *how* exactly we'll meet him. Where is he? What does he look like? How do we see him and follow his progress? How does the scene evolve and become absorbed into the overall flow? Narrative might be best conceived as the camera's eye, telling us what to see and how to feel about it.

Construction is nothing less than the seamless combination of all of these elements. It weaves story into plot and selects the best narrative approach to bring the novel to life. Critically, construction is concerned with an aerial view of the novel – the novel as a blueprint. Construction is the complete orchestration process by which we ensure the reader is drawn into the book, engaged within it, pulled along and brought to a satisfactory conclusion. It deals with chapter structure (if there are chapters), organises the distribution of episodes, monitors pace and generally makes the multiple ingredients work. Almost all of the errors mentioned earlier are caused by faulty construction.

A note on creativity

Much of what follows may look technical, rigid, prescriptive – even manipulative. Many writers don't like to think of writing in this way. Surely imagination, inspiration and the organicism of pure creativity recognise no limits, no structures?

It's not like that. This book is not about writing. It's about what happens *before* or *peripheral to* writing. In creating a plot, choosing a perspective, planning your chapters and honing your storylines, you are laying the foundations for creativity rather than stifling it. Once you begin to write, the work you've done in advance will free you more completely than the unreliable muse or the placebo of inspiration.

Rules are for breaking, but first you must have rules. You might decide to veer from your plans once you begin writing, but at least you'll know how far you've veered and what has to be done to stay on track. You'll have a clear sense of where the reader is supposed to be, and when. In every one of my novels, I've drifted from the path, added new characters, modified storylines and been struck with new, better, ideas. Without a structure in the first place, I would never have had the secure platform for such improvisation.

The immediate challenge

In the last chapter, we saw the process by which an initial idea can attain texture with detail, character, episode, story and theme. These are the raw materials with which we must construct the novel: storylines, plot, narrative approaches, and chapter structures. (Clearly, if you've skipped those earlier phases, you won't have much to work with here.)

Now is when a huge amount of variables come into play. There's so much to consider that it's easy to panic or get lost. You might have multiple storylines in mind, multiple characters and multiple locations. Or you might have just one powerful character and a strong premise to play with.

At this stage, you need to be solidifying what kind of novel you want to write. Your research and planning so far will probably have been taking you in a particular direction, but there may still be a few nagging questions. What you need is a broad framework on which to hang your story.

Zeno's paradox

At the heart of all structural endeavour is a particular way of thinking: the conceptualisation of the novel as a distinct and finite entity. The writer-as-writer – as opposed to the writer-as-reader – must conceive his work from above, as a map or a blueprint that begins as a blank and is filled with detail. Clearly, no architect would begin a building without a blueprint. Every minor mismeasurement or omission would snowball into an eventual structure of catastrophic instability.

The Greek philosopher Zeno of Elea is noted for a so-called paradox that illustrates the challenge. If a man is going to run 100 metres, he must first run 50 metres. To run 50 metres, he must first run 25. To run 25, he must cover 12.5 metres and so on with ever smaller increments that seem to magnify the task beyond the realm of possibility. He has so many stages to pass, he can surely never make it. Of course, he does make it – that's the paradox.

Is the novel any different? It is a finite structure with a beginning and an end. It also has many increments (chapters, scenes, plot points). Understanding the challenge of structure means understanding the parameters in a lucid, objective manner. We must see the whole and its parts always in relation to each other, moving from step to step but always making forward progress to a designated end. This is the framework within which the creative work of narrative will take place.

Organising principles

So it's initially about a framework and identifying some of the potential increments of Zeno's paradox. This means asking a few very generic questions about structure before you begin work on a plot. Different novels will have different organising principles depending on their subject matter and genre. It's worth asking at this early stage what you think might be the organising principle of your book: the framework which best suits your material. What will be the developmental path?

> **Some novel-organising principles**
>
> - A specified time period
> - A particular character arc
> - A premise developed
> - A set number of chapters
> - An allegory explored
> - A definite word count.

There will probably be some crossover, but you have to start somewhere. For example, if you know for certain that your novel takes place over eight months, you can instantly create eight sections (notionally or literally) and begin to populate them with detail from your story-building stage. If you know your initial premise (a man finds a bag of money at a bus stop), you can consider the next five or ten things that happen. If you're thinking about an allegorical novel (an isolated school stands for the whole of society), you can begin to lay out a number of ways in which this allegory is developed. In such simple and tentative ways do you start the process of framework-building.

Now we'll consider some classic organising principles.

How long will your book be?

The first-time novelist is naturally often bewildered by this question. How can one possibly know? We're told that 60,000 words is about the minimum publishers will accept, but what if the word count falls short? Padding it will certainly show.

Having enough raw material is one way to combat this. It's better to write too much and trim later. Another approach is to think mathematically. With my first novel, I calculated that thirty chapters of around 3,000 words each would give me about 90,000 words. It didn't matter if some chapters were shorter and others longer provided I maintained the average. The challenge was then to build a story over thirty consecutive parts. That was one of my organising principles.

Long practice had shown me how many words it typically takes to relate a certain amount of information. I know that a scene in a bar, say, might break down into a brief introduction, a transition, some dialogue, the main body of the action and a link to the next part – perhaps 1,500 words depending on the amount and purpose of the dialogue. Such things are learned only through practice and become instinctive over time, just as journalists become consistently able to write their magazine features to 700 or 1,500 words. In the end, my first book was twenty-seven chapters and 95,000 words. Some chapters were absorbed into others.

There's nothing to stop you plotting your story without chapters. They can be added later and needn't necessarily be of equal length. But beginning without any idea of eventual length is dangerous because it's difficult to have a sense of 'too much' or 'too little'. A notional word count gives you a parameter, which gives you an interior sense of your novel's dimension.

What kind of book will yours be?

Again, you'll have a good idea of this from your previous planning. You probably knew before you even started whether it would be a western or crime thriller or meditation on man's inhumanity to man. Now it's worth thinking very broadly about what kind of structure it might follow. To some extent, this is a question that will already have been answered by genre and subject matter. There are too many possible structures to cover here, but here are some classic simple examples that might help steer your thoughts.

Some plot types

- The quest: a challenge and a search with numerous successive episodes and a prize (or failure).
- The conspiracy: numerous seemingly unconnected storylines begin to weave into one encompassing master thesis.
- The epic: a sprawling canvas of multiple heroic characters engaged in momentous acts.
- The investigation: a mystery presents a series of clues to be followed towards a solution.
- The road trip: classic linear journey during which conflicts are faced and epiphanies had.
- The romance: he loves her; he doesn't love her; he does love her; he loves someone else; he marries her.
- The allegory: the confined space (village, ship, office, island) provides a microcosm of the world.
- The threat: a malign influence arrives, terrorises, is fought and is overcome (or not).
- The farce: a ludicrous situation is established, escalated, played out, and resolved.
- The journey: like the road trip, but with more local colour and detail.
- The plan: people get together to execute a heist/concert/reunion and experience pitfalls or triumphs.
- The screenplay: classic three-act structure (see below).
- The rite of passage: a journey/experience/epiphany that marks a change or growth in personality.

Such categories appear to reduce the novel to mere formulae, and so they do – but these formulae have influenced storytelling since stories existed. It's because they work. Nor are they strictly techniques of genre. What is *Hamlet* if not an investigator looking into the murder of his father? *Lolita* is a murder mystery. *Moby Dick* is a quest. You'll find many more on the internet. The point is that is that there are multiple options to guide the eventual structure of your novel. We need to bear them in mind as we get into the early stages.

Beginning, middle and end

This is your basic framework: your structural starting point. It looks childishly simple as a diagram – so simple, in fact, that many first-time novelists don't consider it in any but the most abstract sense. It's just taken as read. We need to keep this structure firmly at the forefront of our thoughts for a few good reasons.

The **beginning** of the novel has a number of functions. In the first 10–20 per cent of the book, your task is to introduce characters, storylines, tone and narrative perspective in order to

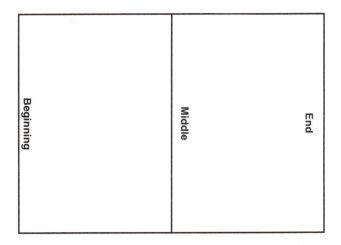

Figure 4.1 The basic novel framework

acclimatise the reader. This is when you hook them and earn their engagement. If you have no idea what the parameters of your book are (how many words, how many chapters, where it ends etc.), how do you know if you've spent too much or too little time establishing your story? How do you know if the book is moving quickly or slowly if you don't know how far away the middle or end is? You'll have to resolve such things in multiple re-writes if you haven't considered them at the start.

The **middle** is just a notional marker. We'd expect the reader to have reached a certain place this far into the novel – a certain level of engagement and interest in the characters and their stories. Think of it in a purely physical sense: the reader is holding a book and they are literally in the middle of it. What has happened so far? We should be literally and figuratively in the middle of the action by now. There might be a revelation or a twist here that changes the whole plot. Again, if you don't know where the middle of your novel is by the time you start writing, how can you manage pace and storylines to keep the reader interested?

The **end** is what the reader is heading for. Whether your book is a genre piece or serious literature, you have to aim your reader at the end and direct all your efforts to making them care about getting there. Some authors have even advocated conceiving the story from its end point and working back to the beginning so that everything happens intuitively and organically. You have to have some idea of not only how your book ends, but also where. Otherwise, how can you build anticipation and time it correctly? In a thriller, you ideally need to be accelerating your story for the last 20–30 per cent of the book, bringing strands together and creating ever greater suspense. The reader can see how many pages are left to the end – you should know as well.

Try drawing the above framework on a piece of paper and mapping some of your existing material on to it. Where would storylines start in relation to each other? When would we meet key characters? When would pivotal episodes occur? Is there an even distribution between the elements you have? Have you got enough material to fill the space? Can you immediately see gaps where you need more story elements?

If more first-time novelists attempted this elementary task, they'd realise that they may not have as much material as they think, that they don't have an aerial view of their book.

> *A story should have a beginning, middle and an end, but not necessarily in that order.*
> Jean-Luc Godard (cited in Felstead, 2014)

Broad movements – the three-act structure

The beginning–middle–end structure is fundamental to storytelling, but it lacks subtlety for something of a novel's scope. There need to be successive levels of structural refinement, establishing a more flexible and adaptable framework for the story. First, a lesson from Hollywood.

Many screenplays follow the so-called 'three-act structure': a basic but effective framework for laying out the plot in way designed to grab the viewer's attention and keep it until the end. It might not suit every kind of novel, but you might benefit from thinking about your own overall structure in similar terms. It's especially useful in books where pace is important (crime, thrillers, mystery).

Used in an unimaginative way, this has undoubtedly produced scores of predictable and poor-quality movies. A structure, after all, is not a replacement for a good story. But then neither is a formal structure a guarantee of bad art. Shakespeare wrote in acts that adhered to accepted norms of dramatic progression. Few would accuse his sonnets of suffering from the limitations of a standard poetic form.

The three-act structure is useful because it reminds us of the necessity of plot points. Something has to be happening at every stage of the book, otherwise there's nothing for the reader to hold on to or engage with. Your challenge as a literary or commercial novelist is to populate a structure in such a way that it seems invisible to the reader. The structure – as an identifiable structure – is for your benefit alone. The reader should notice it only when it isn't there.

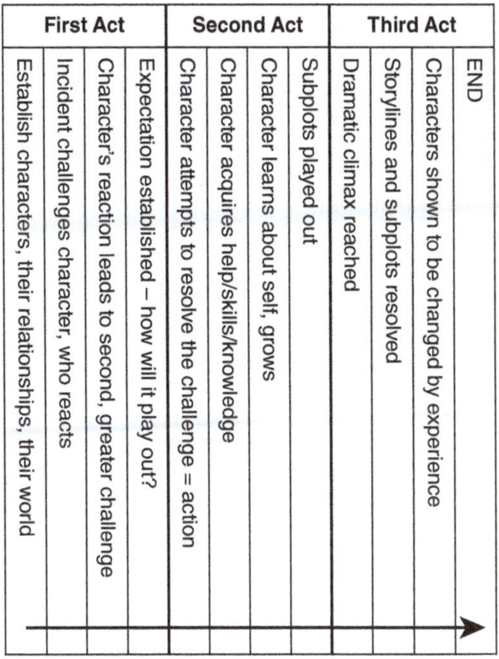

First Act				Second Act				Third Act			
Establish characters, their relationships, their world	Incident challenges character, who reacts	Character's reaction leads to second, greater challenge	Expectation established – how will it play out?	Character attempts to resolve the challenge = action	Character acquires help/skills/knowledge	Character learns about self, grows	Subplots played out	Dramatic climax reached	Storylines and subplots resolved	Characters shown to be changed by experience	END

Figure 4.2 The three-act structure

Plot points are the primary elements of occurrence: the means by which you order all of your research detail, characters, themes, storylines etc. Plotting is the next stage of the structuring process.

Requirements of plot

Naturally, it's more complex than it appears. In populating your structure, you're not just laying out the story in a linear fashion. Simply doing that would lead to a very thin read with relatively little occurrence over the full word count – like trying to make a one-line joke last for fifteen minutes. Before you can start adding all the detail, you need to be aware of what a plot needs to fill a structure.

What makes a plot?

- Plot type (see 'Some plot types' above)
- Broad movements (beginning, middle, end)
- Chronology
- Character combination and character arc
- Storylines – their distribution and juxtaposition
- Plot points and occurrence
- Engagement devices
- Subplots
- Themes and motifs
- Narrative approaches.

Each category has its own considerations and variations. Together, and in seamless combination, they form the matter that fills the structure of your novel. Having looked at the broadest notions of beginning, middle and end, we now move on to the nitty-gritty of how that space is filled.

Chronology

'. . . NOT NECESSARILY IN THAT ORDER'

The three-act structure is typically a start-to-finish chronology, but not every novel is linear. Backstory and flashbacks are common. Some novels move between storylines in different periods. Some (usually the literary) are narrated in reverse or out of order.

Problems occur when the novel chronology is inconsistent or not properly contextualised. For example, I read one student novel that began at a wedding, flashed back via the bride's thoughts and then flashed back again with an omniscient monologue on family history – all on the first page! What is the reader to make of this? Which is the primary storyline? Where's the focus? Where is the actual start of the book?

If you're going to move between time periods, you have a responsibility not only to signpost the boundaries with chapter headings or with character/story threads, but also to ensure that these different temporal strata work consistently and coherently. The reader mustn't feel that they're being jerked from one time to another.

Consider a badly told joke. We all know someone who starts to tell one, misremembers it, goes back to restate the premise, continues, gets the punchline wrong and then retells it. Impact is lost. It's less funny. It doesn't work. Many first-time novels read in just this manner.

Of course, there are notable examples of multiple digressions and reversals being effective. Comedian Ronnie Corbett used to do a skit on TV where he seemed inadvertently to wander ever further from his initial premise, taking the viewer on a picaresque comic journey that came back to the start. *Tristram Shandy* is a masterpiece of digressive narrative, in which the protagonist takes two volumes even to get born – the point being that the point never seems to get made. Such things are very difficult to do.

Below, we'll consider some standard structural approaches to chronology, their advantages and their pitfalls. First, a look at some perennial pairs.

Prologues and epilogues

Prologues sometimes have a bad name. This is because they are occasionally used in a way that seems unnecessary and which serves only to delay the start of the principal storyline. Often, they might as well just be first chapters.

A prologue needs to justify its existence by providing a significant pre-story context or getting round a tricky structural requirement. Examples of these might be:

- An event that takes place before the main action and which lends colour or meaning to everything that follows. An alternative option here is to drip-feed the same information in character flashbacks or narrative backstory, so you need to decide which works better. The former drops all the context into one place, where it can gradually fade from memory as the reader progresses. This could be useful if you want the reader to be surprised when an old detail re-emerges. The latter option could work better for dramatic irony, juxtaposing present action with past context more consistently and drawing dramatic parallels.

- An event drawn from later on in the action – often the middle or the end. Typically, this shows us the protagonist triumphant, in the midst of a tricky situation, down on his luck or in a high-action scene. This sets up reader expectation and generates questions from the start. How did the character get there? What was the route he took? How will he get out of it? The technique also offers you the chance to kick off with some real pace if you know it'll take a while to establish a series of complex storylines or cast of characters. You buy yourself time by promising action further on and by creating a loop whereby the reader gets a satisfying connection when the narrative catches up.

In my novel *The Vice Society*, I have a prologue in which we see a woman fall from the Monument in London and the inquest following her death. This provides an immediate focus for the reader and allows me to suck them into the world of Victorian London. Chapter 1 begins seven years later and kicks off a handful of chapters in which I have to establish a broad cast of characters. Only in Chapter 6 is a strong connection made back to the events of the prologue.

In another (as yet unpublished) novel called *The Lost Archipelagos*, I was telling the story of a sea voyage. I didn't want to kick off the story with a prologue set in London, where the voyage began, because this was not to be a London book. It was to be an exotic piece set entirely in the Pacific Ocean. For this reason, I decided to set Chapter 1 in a storm at Cape Horn, thereby establishing the tone and setting of the book with a pacey and atmospheric scene. Fortuitously, it used to take vessels a minimum of three weeks to go round the Horn, so this gave me the opportunity to leave the crew in peril and use Chapter 2 to flash back to London and the novel's premise. Chapter 3 saw the ship safely round the Horn and the action continued in linear fashion for the next sixty chapters.

Epilogues may have a worse reputation than prologues. If something hasn't been said in the course of the narration, why say it afterwards? Surely it's redundant. The epilogue is therefore best used as a sort of echo: a 'what happened next' feature that looks into the future of characters and storylines.

It might be that the action of the novel has shown us only a fragment – a disproportionate and unrepresentative section – of a character's life or of a historical period. Normality resumes in the epilogue: after the action is over. Or it might be that the conclusion reached in the novel's dénouement is a fragile one, unstable and certain to change. The epilogue deals with the powerful expectation of subsequent events. Comedic crime writer Carl Hiaasen sometimes ends his books with a brief round-up of what each character did next – an entertaining way to show who got their comeuppance, who was rewarded and who lived happily ever after.

Again, it's necessary to consider the difference between a final chapter and an epilogue. Sometimes, the only material difference is what you choose to call it, but readers do have different expectations depending on how the section is labelled. Thrillers often have a chapter that appears after the climax has been reached. It shows us the spy or the hero relaxing on a beach, being debriefed, or walking epically alone into the hills. These are not epilogues – they follow the action more or less directly.

Flashback and backstory

What's the difference? I'd say a flashback is presented from the character's point of view, whereas backstory is handled by the narrator (the author, or a controlling voice in the story) as part of the more formal business of structure. A flashback may be an element of backstory, but may also add a necessary bit of context. Both play important parts in the handling of storylines. The challenge arises in how and where you insert these backward glances.

The common error is to disrupt narrative flow by distracting the reader from the principal timeline with seemingly intrusive 'contextualising'. This can be avoided by establishing the main storyline(s) early on – acclimatising the reader – and leading into absorbed backstory/flashback later, or by separating timeframes quite distinctly into their own chapters. Each option has its own benefits and drawbacks.

Absorbed – the flashback/backstory appears within the general flow of the narrative and within chapters. This allows relevant detail to be dropped in always at the most opportune moment, emphasising or juxtaposing as required. The challenge is organising this so that the reader doesn't feel alienated from the immediate action and so the flashbacks don't appear too pointed in their purpose.

For example, in my first book, *The Incendiary's Trail*, I have a nameless, unspeaking prisoner in a cell. His interrogators can get nothing out of him, except to deduce from his appearance who and what he might be. When they leave him alone in his cell, the narrator takes over and tells the reader part of his backstory. As the book goes on, we see more parts of this story at opportune moments (when the character is alone, thinking) until the whole of his backstory is revealed. The alternative would be . . .

Separate – the flashback/backstory appears in its own space, with its own chapters or prologue. This allows a larger amount of information to appear in one place, but with the concomitant threat of establishing a rival narrative thread. Is this one story or two? The spaces between the principal storyline and the flash-backs/backstory have to be managed carefully or else one (or both) may start to seem less relevant.

For example, in my novel *The Lost Archipelagos*, I could have referred to the London episode (Chapter 2) in many small flash-backs throughout the novel. This would have allowed me more pace at the start. However, the novel was one of relentless for-ward motion – a sea voyage – and to keep flashing back would have detracted from the immediate time and place. On balance, it worked better in a separate place.

Films are usually a good example of effective ways to handle flash-back/backstory because cinema relies so heavily on forward motion. A film doesn't stop, so the viewer should never be in a position where they have to stop and think. Watch a few films and note when the chronology changes, how the switch is effected and how long it lasts.

Structural chronology

Of course, it's about more than the occasional flashback or con-textualising backstory. Sometimes you're dealing with multiple storylines that run in different timeframes. The challenge here is balancing them so that they work with, not against, each other.

Let's say you have a novel with two main storylines: one in Revolutionary France and one in the present day. Figure 4.3 below shows one way this might be handled. The columns are alternating chapters, the shaded ones being those in the past. How well would this work?

The first thing to say is that it looks very mechanical. A reader would be flipping from one story to the other in a very predictable manner. To work well, the two storylines would have to be connected to each other in a compelling manner, otherwise we'd just be reading two shorter, separate, books interleaved like decks of cards. One chapter would have to reflect, prefigure or otherwise inform the next, which is actually an advantage in terms of pace because the reader would always be looking back and forward. If time travel were part of the story, a character familiar to both storylines could form the link. Alternatively, the two stories may deal with analogous themes: a witch-hunt in the past, a racism trial in the present.

The past/present storyline seems to be quite popular among first-time novelists. Alas, two major pitfalls (other than the chronological challenge) accompany it. The first is that the writer tends to be more interested in one of the two storylines, with the result that the favoured one is better and therefore draws the reader's attention to the extent that the other is skipped. The second pitfall is the decision to write a book of two periods in an attempt to bolster word count by fitting two novels into one. Alas, that's how it usually reads.

What if the shaded chapters represented not another storyline but flashbacks from the main story? That would be exceptionally maddening and ill-advised.

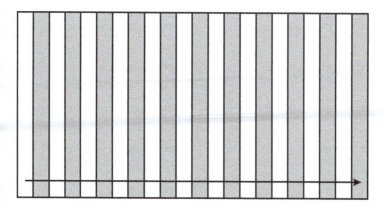

Figure 4.3 Alternating-chapter chronology

If the same past/present story were written according to the image below (Figure 4.4), how would it be different?

At first sight, this looks less busy, less frenetic in its changes of focus. However, the distance between the two storylines threatens to make one seem irrelevant while reading the other. It's actually more difficult to keep some connection if there are too many pages in between. Moreover, the first few chapters concentrate on one storyline, implying that this is the primary one. When the second one kicks in, the reader is left confused, having spent a few pages buying into the first. The same situation would occur if one storyline occupied a solid third, or half, or quarter of the book. It would seem oddly irrelevant, an add-on or a bit of filler.

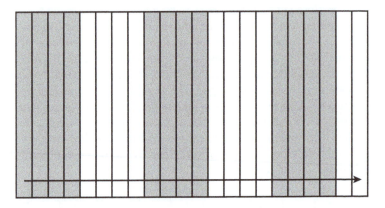

Figure 4.4 Block-chapter chronology

Until now, we've been considering different chronological storylines. What if there's one story thread but with different time periods? The easiest option would be to tell the story in order, stepping from period to period as in David Nicholls' *One Day*. This makes for a well-paced read and a logical narrative flow, but the benefit of juxtaposition is mostly accumulative and from one chapter to the next. A more literary option might present a storyline out of order as in Figure 4.5 below.

In this version, we see the story of a single character (or a group of them) over a few decades, moving back and forth between

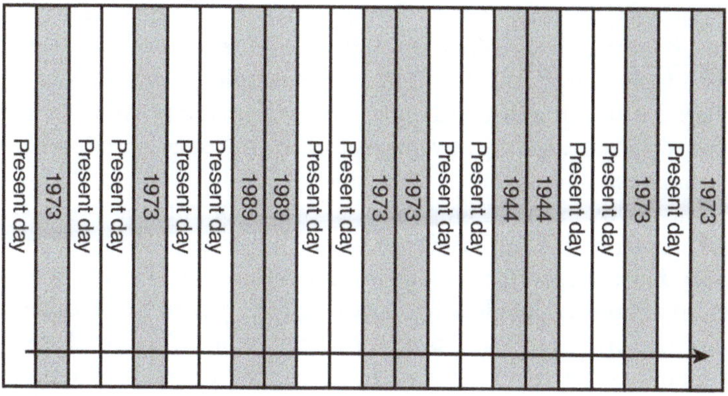

Figure 4.5 Interchangeable-chapter chronology

periods. Each storyline is consecutive within its period, and within the chapter structure, but not in the overall chronology of the story. It's a trickier read, but arguably more engaging for the reader because there are multiple juxtapositions and connections, both forwards and backwards in time. The chronology is a puzzle that will be solved only by finishing the book. Not only this, but the author gets to play with his cast of characters and collection of themes over a broader canvas. So much will change.

Naturally, such a plot is quite tricky to work out, but it illustrates the advantages and pitfalls associated with novel chronology. The permutations are manifold, but the considerations remain much the same: how do you engineer the relationships between periods so that they contribute most effectively with each other? How do you order chronology to manage pace and sense?

Such broad, chronological divisions are not the only ones. Sometimes it's fun to play with minor time slippages. A common enough technique is to take the reader to a particular point in the story (the assassin with his finger on the trigger, the bride about to say 'I do') and pause the narrative to go back a few steps before catching up again. This might happen within a chapter and need not take a large part of the structure.

In my third book, *The Thieves' Labyrinth*, I paused the action in one chapter and literally wound back the story so that the horses trotted backwards through the streets to where they'd come from. After I'd filled in that brief subplot, I flicked back to where I'd begun and carried on. This was made possible by the whimsical narrator and by the nature of the series itself, which was interested in narrative techniques.

The following is a simplified schematic of the chronological arrangement of *Lolita*. The entire story is told in past-tense retrospect, but there are broad timeframes within this. Thus, the first eleven chapters provide a backstory to the character of Humbert before he arrives in Ramsdale. We then have a sort of condensed, 'catching-up' chapter written in the present tense in which Humbert summarises the progress of his initial infatuation with Lolita. Then the novel continues in a straightforward direction to a point in Part Two where it's necessary for time to speed up so that Humbert can visit Lolita as an older girl. Thereafter, standard forward chronology takes over. It should also be noted that there are mentions within past sections of future occurrences (i.e. the Humbert of Chapter 3 might compare a character of his past to Lolita in a future chapter because the whole book is in retrospect). We'll come to this later when we discuss story structure.

Chapters 1–10	Chapter 11	Novel mid-section	Part Two Chapters 25–28	To conclusion
Humbert's past up to Ramsdale, including childhood and first marriage	Humbert's present-tense diary in Ramsdale	Regular forward chronology	'Next three years' – montage	Regular forward chronology

Figure 4.6 Chronological divisions in *Lolita*

Another way of conceiving chronology is a simple line. This works better if you're not yet able to picture your book in terms of chapters. Just draw a line showing the forward motion of your story and indicate where the story looks back.

In Figure 4.7, a sample book begins at the start (S) and proceeds in the standard forward direction (even if the story is all told in retrospect) and flashes back twice to a time before the story began before continuing on its way. *The Vice Society* begins with a prologue set in a period before the start of the story as related in the book. *Lolita* has but four paragraphs of the major (retrospective) storyline before flashing back to Humbert's backstory. Later on in the book, three years are explained away or condensed in a sort of montage summary section. Such diagrams are not 'to scale' or accurate in any way that might seriously aid later attempts at structure, but they do allow you to begin visualising your novel in your own way. I've always wondered if such a narrative line might be drawn for Ford Maddox Ford's phenomenally complex chronology in *The Good Soldier*. I'd like to see it.

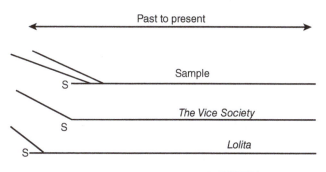

Figure 4.7 Timeline examples

The narrative calendar

Something that many first-time novelists don't consider is the precise duration of their story: the number of days or weeks or years that it spans. You might have a character reading a newspaper on Tuesday, and three chapters later it's Tuesday again. Have seven days actually passed? Was there enough incident to fill that time?

Publishers usually employ a copy-editor to trawl through your text and check all the dates and times to ensure they add up. This only happens if you've already secured a publishing contract, however, so it's a good idea to spend some time working it out for yourself. Personally, I write the story first, paying greatest attention to the action and engagement. Only afterwards do I go through and work out what period I've actually covered. It usually proves necessary to change a few days or amend a few sentences to suit.

The 'narrative calendar' is particularly important in books that deal with stepped processes: an investigation, a trial, a journey. If the chronology doesn't work out, the perspicacious reader will be sending you a letter saying something like, 'Maureen planted her tomatoes on Tuesday morning but Derek was eating them only two days later. This is agriculturally impossible because . . . '

It's easy to joke about it, but these things are important. Invariably, a quick chronological check will show where the weaknesses in your novel lie. Stephen King tells a story about how, when writing *Cujo*, he had to go back and rewrite large parts of it because he'd miscalculated the incubation period of rabies. The initial narrative span didn't reflect the reality.

Character

Two broad schools of thought suggest that novels are character-driven or plot-driven. It might be useful for you to decide which approach you're taking with your book. A plot-driven novel might originate with a powerful premise, a storyline, a location or a genre and draw in characters as required. For example, if your novel closely follows the events of the Great Fire of London, you might begin with a solid sense of the chronology and events before selecting a necessary cast to bring it alive. Alternatively, you might decide to write a novel based around students sharing a house. There's no particular overarching storyline here; rather, you begin with a good cast of characters whose varying personalities and motivations will generate their own storylines. In the Great Fire option, the events compel character activity; in the student house, character compels plot.

This is, of course, a simplification. Good, well-drawn characters will always suggest storylines, just as good storylines will always suggest good characters. The point is that you, as author, keep a solid sense of how you use character to start building your book before you start writing.

Character is certainly one of the key structural elements to consider. It's through the characters that we experience most of the action. They provide the conduits for the reader's empathy and engagement. They also provide an organisational challenge: the plot must be divided among them in such a way that all are consistently involved and coherently part of the storylines. Like sheep, they must be herded lest they wander off. They must always be kept within structural sight.

Two organising principles present themselves. The first is the character's own storyline, perhaps better understood as their 'arc'. The second is what and how they contribute to the overall cast. The latter is where we'll start.

The character mix

A novel is an ensemble piece whose texture comes partially from character interplay. We follow the stories of an individual, but we derive pleasure from how those stories interweave, collide with or juxtapose the stories of others. Think of them as musical instruments which must play together in the symphony of plot. Some may take the dominant role (the piano, the lead violin) while others provide light relief (the harp, the piccolo). Your role as author is to compose before you conduct.

Consider the illustration below of the principal characters in *Hamlet*. Literature students may disagree with some of my summaries, but you'll see at a glance that as well as each character having their own role, they also provide a spectrum through which Hamlet himself is viewed.

For example, Laertes is a young man returning to his studies. He worries about his sister and defers to his father Polonius. He is also a foil to Hamlet: Hamlet under other circumstances – a noble young student with a stable family and a firm sense of honour. When Laertes acts, he shows up Hamlet's indecision.

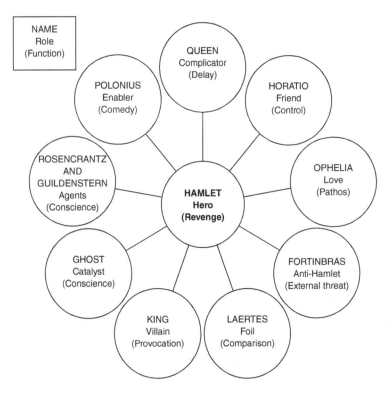

NAME
Role
(Function)

QUEEN
Complicator
(Delay)

POLONIUS
Enabler
(Comedy)

HORATIO
Friend
(Control)

ROSENCRANTZ
AND
GUILDENSTERN
Agents
(Conscience)

HAMLET
Hero
(Revenge)

OPHELIA
Love
(Pathos)

GHOST
Catalyst
(Conscience)

FORTINBRAS
Anti-Hamlet
(External threat)

KING
Villain
(Provocation)

LAERTES
Foil
(Comparison)

Figure 4.8 Character mix in *Hamlet*

Or consider the Ghost, who is a necessary catalyst in kicking off the story (revealing his murder) and who appears later to prick Hamlet's conscience.

The characters and their relationships form a narrative tissue that lends texture to the plot. To follow one is to be aware of others through comparison. The model is relatively simple in *Hamlet* because one character is at the core and the rest are subsidiary. They do have relationships with each other (Polonius/Laertes/ Ophelia, the king and queen) but these are subordinate to their relationships with Hamlet. In a novel, you may have a number of core characters who relate to each other and who have their own satellite cast. The cast of characters sets up multiple connections, some of which may be reflected in the plot, some of which exist purely to flesh out the characters and make them real.

Your role as structuring author is to weave your cast through the other elements of plot: storyline, chronology, theme, pace, etc. Here is an image showing character relation in my novel *The Vice Society*:

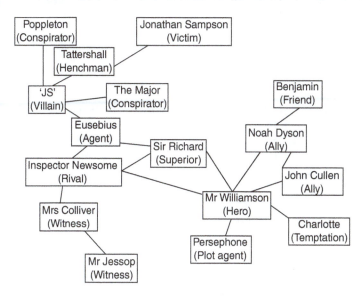

Figure 4.9 Character mix in *The Vice Society*

This diagram is different from the one in Chapter 3, Building Story, though the book is the same. Here, our connections are strictly between characters and suggest different stories from those in the ideas map. Even a cursory study shows that we have 'baddies', 'goodies', victims, witnesses and agents to move between them. All are connected in single or multiple ways and play off each other. It might be discerned that there are two distinct sides to the story and this is indeed the case. Sir Richard stands pivotally at the centre as Commissioner of Police while Mr Williamson and Inspector Newsome pursue the same case from two different angles. There is also a third strand in which the villains are connected to the police via the double agent Eusebius.

Sometimes it's the story that brings the cast together to provide occurrence; sometimes pre-existing or peripheral relationships lend texture. For example, the rivalry between Mr Williamson and Inspector Newsome flavours much of the action as they compete to solve a crime, but Mr Williamson's experiences with the prostitute Charlotte have little to do with the meat of the plot. It's just character work.

Minor characters do not feature in the diagram because they are generally mere agents of plot – they exist to provide key information, to die conveniently and to lend local colour. Such characters are often the most fun to write because they require little depth or responsibility. They embellish the novel as brief flashes of wit and add further to overall effect. They burn brightly, but only briefly. Dickens was a master of the minor character, many of whom probably deserved a novel of their own (would you rather have a drink with drippy and wholesome little Oliver Twist or with Cockney chancer the Artful Dodger?). In *The Vice Society*, I introduced a filthy and malicious street urchin called Roger – a minor character I liked so much that I brought him back in a later book.

It's a curious fact that the peripheral characters are sometimes the most convincing or engaging in many first novels. My belief is that this stems from the lack of pressure they put on the author. A main character has to carry so much weight, but a walk-on need only fulfil an immediate and easily identifiable role. It's as if they write themselves because their plot function is so clear. There is a lesson here.

Below is a diagram of the major characters (shaded) of *The Vice Society* and the minor characters I employed to aid their passage through the plot. The minor characters are people they interrogate, people they meet who tell them things, or people who stand in their way. Most of them were suggested by necessity and as such were answers to the questions of the story-building process (e.g. 'How can Mr Newsome find out about the importance of the pomegranate seeds found at the murder scene?').

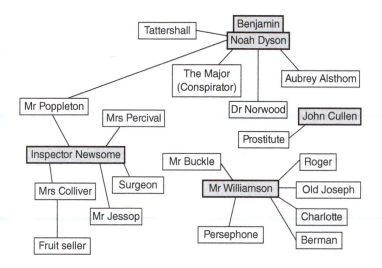

Figure 4.10 Relation of major and minor characters in *The Vice Society*

For example, Mr Jessop heard the accident that led to the fall from the window, Roger witnessed a murder in a slum and Mr Buckle is used to emphasise Mr Williamson's initial impotence. They're all walk-on parts, but essential to the movement of the story.

The main thing to remember about the character mix is that it acts as glue on the rest of the plot elements. Everything in a successful novel is organically connected to everything else. Any character who's not playing their part (whether instrumental or decorative) is surplus to requirements. The editor of my first novel wondered if I might cut a recurring minor character because he never spoke or contributed anything in terms of occurrence. The character was one of a crowd of malformed people in a travelling freak show and in this case I argued for his survival because I thought he added a certain horrifying presence to the overall visual effect. He stayed, but it was a valid debate.

The ideal situation is that the reader comes to know your characters and their inter-relationships sufficiently well that he begins to anticipate outcomes based on individual personalities and stories. When the reader sees that X and Y are going to meet in the next chapter, he thinks, 'Ooh, there'll be fireworks then!' or 'Oh no! What if she lets slip she slept with his brother?' In this way is the reader pulled in and the novel given depth.

Character arc and line

Each of the major characters has their own stake and role in the broader storylines, driving and originating events or reacting to them as they occur. It should be possible – and this is a good editing tip – to read through a novel looking at one (major) character only and still find a coherent story. It might not be the story of the book as a whole, but it will be inextricably interwoven. To go back to the orchestral comparison, each character is contributing an instrument to the overall score.

Each major character also has an arc, which follows their experience of the story but which is in some ways peripheral to it. Their arc is their storyline *plus* their psychological responses to it. For example, my detective Mr Williamson is a conflicted man whose strict morality becomes ever more at odds with the circumstances of his life. He finds that he must sometimes break the law to uphold it. When he questions a prostitute, he is forced to fight feelings he would rather deny. Such inner conflict follows him throughout the various occurrences of the storyline, asking the reader to empathise with him as well as observing how he investigates the crime.

The complexity of the arc depends on the kind of book you're writing. Genre fiction tends to favour occurrence over character depth, whereas literary fiction may be more interested in the arc than in narrative movement. Either way, character arc and line is another important consideration of structure.

Both elements – the individual storyline and the arc – are essential to structural texture. They create reader engagement, aid credibility and reinforce the need to read on. It's important, therefore, to ensure that your characters are portrayed consistently throughout the plot. You can't leave them for too long before returning, otherwise their development will not be fluid and the reader may infer that they're not important. You also need to bear in mind the previous point about the character mix, ensuring that the line and arc of one character plays off others.

The diagram below shows the major character spread (who appears when) in the first twenty-one chapters of *The Vice Society*. What strikes you immediately about it?

Even without any indication of story, it should be clear who the major players are. There are patterns here. Note the regularity with which the major characters appear and how other characters appear in relation to them. We're establishing individual character storylines for the first nine chapters, but then they begin to blend. By Chapter 14 (which was initially plotted to be the middle of the book), the various storylines have become fully intertwined and continue like this to the climax in Chapter 27.

From this diagram, the story could be almost anything. It was the same with the ideas maps and is the same with chronology. These are structural elements that go through the story to add texture and consistency. They do not replace story – they allow it to live by supplying other essential elements.

Chapter				
21	Newsome	Mayne		
20	Noah	Cullen		
19	Williamson	Noah	Cullen	Benjamin
18	Eusebius	JS	Benjamin	Cullen
17	Newsome			
16	Williamson	Benjamin	JS	
15	Noah	The Major	Tattershall	
14	Newsome	Williamson	Noah	Eusebius
13	Williamson	Noah	Benjamin	Newsome
12	Mrs Coliver	Tattershall	Newsome	Mayne
11	Williamson	Noah	Benjamin	
10	Newsome	Eusebius	Cullen	JS
9	Williamson	Charlotte		
8	Newsome	Mayne		
7	Williamson	Charlotte		
6	Williamson			
5	Williamson			
4	Eusebius	JS		
3	Newsome	Cullen		
2	Williamson			
1	Newsome	Mayne		
P	Williamson			

Figure 4.11 Chapter–character distribution in *The Vice Society*

Here's the same structure but showing only Mr Williamson's arc:

P	Williamson (wife's death)
1	
2	Williamson (career stasis)
3	
4	
5	Williamson (still got the gift)
6	Williamson (still mourning)
7	Williamson (lacks authority – is frustrated)
8	
9	Williamson (awkward and frustrated – help!)
10	
11	Williamson (gets help – is stronger)
12	
13	Williamson (more in control – feeling stronger)
14	Williamson (conflict – old rivalry with Newsome)
15	
16	Williamson (happier – making progress)
17	
18	
19	Williamson (now part of an effective team)
20	
21	

Figure 4.12 Mr Williamson's character arc in *The Vice Society*

Again, these elements run alongside the story but are not themselves parts of the story. Many other things happen in these chapters and many other relationships are explored (with Noah, with Charlotte, with Mr Cullen). This is simply Mr Williamson's personal path: one of many different threads that form the novel's texture. We're also simultaneously following the arcs of those others that Mr Williamson is interacting with.

Following the logic of the character arc, the initial chapters of your novel must serve the critical function of introducing major characters to the reader. Only when the reader understands the character and their situation can empathy (or any other feeling) turn into engagement. You have to make the reader care. Thus, we see Mr Williamson at a loose end, still a great detective, mourning and frustrated in his attempts to solve the resurgent mystery of his wife's death. Here is a man who needs help and the reader is compelled to feel the same. That way, when help arrives, the reader is satisfied.

The Vice Society has a suite of major characters, which naturally influences the structure it takes. A book with fewer characters might feature all characters in all chapters and be divided according to plot occurrence, or chronology or location. As in David Nicholls' *One Day*, it might be the same people meeting over and over but at different times and places. That's when other elements of structure come to into play.

Let's look at the same sort of thing in *Lolita*:

Chapters 1–10	Chapters 11–33	Part Two 1–24	Part Two 25–27	Part Two 28–29	Part Two 30–end
Humbert Annabel Lee Valeria (Quilty) Charlotte Lolita	Humbert Lolita Charlotte	Lolita Humbert Gaston Godin Mrs Pratt Mona Dahl (Quilty) (Trapp)	Rita Humbert (Trapp)	Lolita Humbert (Quilty) Dick	Humbert Quilty

Figure 4.13 Character distribution in *Lolita*

As is more typical in literature, the novel is structured in broader movements than alternating chapters (the literary novel doesn't need to move so quickly; it can take its time). Humbert is clearly the most consistent character (he's telling the story) and really the only one who has an arc. That arc, as shown in this image, is: backstory and psychological background; meeting and falling for Lolita; running off cross-country with Lolita before stopping at Beardsley College; losing Lolita and stumbling in the wilderness; finding Lolita again; avenging himself against the man who took Lolita from him – all through the retrospective lens of writing from a prison cell.

Lolita is the next most important as the focus of his infatuation. Note that the character of Quilty is also reasonably consistent throughout, though he often appears only by mention, or in person but without a name attached (the parenthetical instances). This is a necessity of plot: Quilty must be a shadowy presence throughout, but not so much that he draws attention to himself as the eventual victim of the murder. This 'blind spot' is aided by Humbert's unreliable first-person narration – he 'misses' clues that the reader sees. Trapp is a figment of Humbert's suspicions.

Storylines

The character/story conundrum is very much like the chicken/egg conundrum. It depends partly on where your idea came from and how you developed it. By the time you get to plotting, however, there should be a healthy interplay between the two: characters suggesting storylines and storylines requiring characters.

Storylines are perhaps the most essential element of construction. Without them, it's debatable whether you've written a novel or just a conglomeration of scenes. Story is the skeleton on which hang the flesh and organs of your novel. It is the primary mechanism by which you pull the reader page by page towards the end. Some might say it's the reason people pay their money in the first place – certainly there are bestsellers whose writing is too abysmal to appeal in its own right.

How many storylines?

A common mistake in first novels is insufficient story to support the word count. This may be one instance of the short story being an unreliable gauge of readiness to write a novel. It stands to reason that, when you're writing around 100,000 words, you need to have plenty of stuff happening.

At the risk of oversimplifying, there are two broad approaches you might take to storylines:

1   Use **just one storyline** and ensure that it delivers sufficient levels of interest from multiple occurrences, pleasing digressions,

powerful characters, or a distinctive narrative voice. The main requirement here is to keep the reader's attention throughout a storyline that is relatively simple. Both *Lolita* and *Moby Dick* have singular storylines. In the former, Humbert Humbert meets the 'nymphet' Lolita and runs off with her on an odyssey of immoral lust after her mother's fortuitous death. In the latter, the sailor Ishmael joins a whaler whose unbalanced captain takes the ship across the Pacific in search of the white whale. The storylines could not be simpler. What makes them great books is everything that happens along the way – or rather, not what happens but the dense fabric of thought and observation that surrounds what happens. Nabokov can fill three pages with a paean to Lolita's tennis game while the story waits politely to continue. Unfortunately, this kind of storyline is probably the more difficult for the first-time novelist because it takes a certain assuredness with your own voice and the ability to free-associate on a theme. It's phenomenally difficult to write ten pages in which nothing really happens but which grip the reader all the same. Better to learn how to walk the tightrope before you go across it on a unicycle while juggling.

2   Use **multiple storylines** and ensure that the reader is always engaged by moving between narratives. This approach sets up plot as a kind of puzzle in which the various pieces are artfully juxtaposed and reading becomes a kind of game in which the reader watches it all come together. It tends to be used in genre books and 'page-turners' because it creates an environment where the reader is always working to make connections. There is always a call to deduce, infer, connect and anticipate. To stop reading is to break momentum and miss something you've been compelled to want.

Multiple storylines may seem trickier to create, but they turn out easier for most writers because they offer more to work with and more to structure. Each major character (or time period) can have a distinct storyline and so you might actually end up writing a number of sub-novels within the larger frame, which takes the pressure off. You also have to make them connect, but we'll come to that.

What is a storyline?

Another apparently obvious question, and another one that's usually not considered because it seems so simple. The 'line' part is important. If the story is a summary of the action, a storyline is in many ways a microcosm of the novel as a whole. It must have a contextualising beginning, a rational and organic development and a satisfying end. It is also typically allied to one or more character arcs and must also work harmoniously alongside parallel storylines.

There are a number of storylines in *The Vice Society*:

1   Ex-detective George Williamson receives a pseudonymous letter telling him that his wife's suicide seven years before was murder and that the solution to this crime is the same as a case being investigated by Williamson's arch-rival and erstwhile boss Inspector Albert Newsome. No longer a serving policeman, Williamson must enlist the help of two shady characters he knows to help him investigate the truth of the letter.

2   Inspector Albert Newsome is investigating what appears to be a fatal fall from a window. As he looks further into the case, he begins to discover connections to the pornographic book trade and to certain powerful men. Then he finds out that Mr Williamson – a better detective – is investigating the same case.

3   The Society for the Suppression of Vice is a charitable organisation which is against public immorality. When the fatal fall occurs on Holywell Street – a notorious centre of pornographic book printing – the society puts pressure on the Metropolitan Police to solve the crime quickly and even offers help in the form of one of its spies, Eusebius Bean. But is the Vice Society's real interest in solving the crime or in covering it up?

These three broad storylines (and their subplots, which we'll consider later) direct the entire action of the book. It's clear from their summaries that all are interconnected. You'll also see that they are bound up with certain character arcs.

For comparison, my novel *The Lost Archipelagos* has a single storyline:

> A captain is engaged to take a group of eccentric old men to the furthest reaches of the uncharted Pacific. During the voyage, the initial reasons given for the trip are revealed as lies and the true objective turns out to be something darker and far more fantastic. The further the ship and crew travel, the stranger the action becomes. It is essentially a book of episodes and themes organised around the linear momentum of a journey. (Homer's *Odyssey* is the same kind of thing.)

In both single- and multiple-storyline novels, there will additionally be numerous stories or subplots within the broader storyline strands. These might be whole chapters, episodes, asides, digressions or contextualising flashbacks. They provide dimension to the novel as a whole. A book like Homer's *Odyssey* is full of such stories (Circe, the Cyclops, Calypso), which are entertaining in their own right but which all work towards the overall storyline of the hero returning home to Ithaca. Many of the Bible's stories are similarly memorable.

Once you have a storyline (and characters, and an idea of what type of book, its projected length, and sense of chronology) it's time to really get started on the complexities of plot.

Plotting storylines

One paradox of plotting is that it's not about simply laying out the storylines. It's about manipulating the storylines in such a way that you introduce, divide, withhold and reveal with the aim of creating maximum reader engagement. The chronology of the story is not necessarily the same as the chronology of plot.

For example, the *Vice Society* storyline I described above began with Mr Williamson receiving a letter. In the actual book, that happens on page 80. Why? Because the significance of that event requires a prior contextual foundation before it matters to the reader. This is the essence of plot: arranging and combining storylines for maximum effect. In *Lolita*, Humbert mentions his nymphet in the first paragraph but doesn't actually meet her until Chapter 10. Nabokov wants to make us wait.

The complexity of the task depends on numerous factors: how many storylines you have, how many characters, how many chronological changes. We'll begin with the multiple-storyline novel and consider the singe-storyline novel second.

Multiple storylines

Three immediate tasks present themselves with the multiple-storyline novel:

1   How do you introduce them?
2   How do you balance them against each other throughout the novel?
3   How do you combine them into one narrative (if required)?

Beginning can be tricky. The instinctive urge of the first-time novelist is to rush the reader into the plot and tell them everything right away. Characters and storylines tumble over each other, backstories or flashbacks interrupt the forward motion and a narrative traffic jam ensues. This is classic writing-as-a-reader behaviour.

In fact, readers are far more patient than we imagine. As the author, you dictate the pace and manner by which the novel proceeds. Give readers enough to engage them, and they will rightly anticipate that more is to come (they are reading as readers).

The temptation to introduce all storylines simultaneously – though possible – may not always be the best idea. For the sake of argument, though, you might choose to kick off your novel with a hectic scene in which all of your characters and storylines are present. It might be a party at which everyone is present and where all objectives/motivations are revealed to the reader. It could work. It might be one of those prologues that flashes forward.

But it would have to be handled very delicately. There wouldn't have been time to contextualise anything or establish character, and so the next few chapters would have to be used to explain the detail retrospectively. Would pace be lost in going back to fill in the blanks? You might get a third of the way into the book before you've begun all of your storylines properly. More importantly, there might be a nagging sense of catching up that prevents forward motion. As I say, it's possible, but needs some careful consideration.

An alternative is to begin each of the storylines separately. The result here is that the reader has to get to grips with numerous different situations and sets of characters and hold them all in mind until the next storyline instalment lands. Most readers are quite used to this and will go with it. One possible disadvantage is that a novel requiring swift pace may feel a little slow at the start. This could be remedied with a flash forward from one storyline or by keeping the chapters shorter. In any case, most reader will give you a bit of leeway in establishing your storylines.

The diagram below is a representation of the first twenty-odd chapters of *The Vice Society*. Each column is a chapter (prologue included) and each number represents a different character storyline. What are you able to deduce from the diagram?

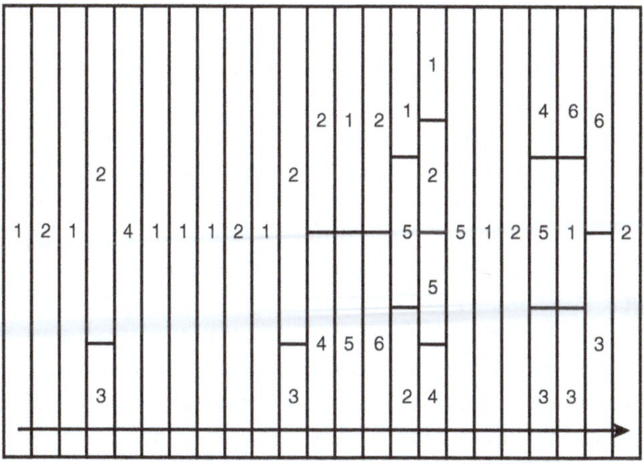

Figure 4.14 Character–storyline distribution in *The Vice Society*

What appears clear is that the initial ten or so chapters focus on the three main storylines, giving each time to develop, but not leaving one for too long without returning. Shorter or longer chapters help in refining this. The number three character (Mr Cullen) does not actually get his own story until after the halfway point, but is recorded here for reference.

By the halfway point, storylines are beginning to blend, with multiple strands occurring in one chapter. Chapter 14 is the one in which the two major character storylines meet (when Newsome and Williamson speak about their respective investigations) and then the storylines partially separate again from here.

It's important to stress again that the plot was designed in this way for a few reasons. As mentioned above, it's necessary to lay the foundation work for the characters and their stories. Who are they? What are they like? What do they want? What stands in their way? What is at stake in the novel as a whole? In the most basic sense: why should the reader care about continuing? If they stopped reading at Chapter 6, what would they be missing?

The initial separation of storylines also invites readers to see the parallels between them, thus creating certain juxtapositional ironies whereby the reader can see what the characters cannot. The narrative high ground set up by the author gives the reader an aerial view – a privileged view – of the action. As the plot moves on, the reader should yearn more and more for the threads to coalesce and for the expected conflicts/revelations/explosions to occur. Everything is orchestrated.

The Vice Society has quite large chapters (3,500 words on average) and chapter length is certainly an important factor. They need to be long enough to serve their purpose, but not so long that they slow initial pace or make the different storylines seem disparate. This was a problem I faced in my book *Holiday Nightmare*, which has eight storylines. I got round this by writing it in 'fragments' of 500–2,500 words, each one revealing only a small part of its respective storyline. The distance between them was therefore not divisive and instead created a greater sense of pace, especially as most of the storylines were connected at multiple points. The diagram for the first half of the book looks like this (each column a fragment, each letter a character storyline):

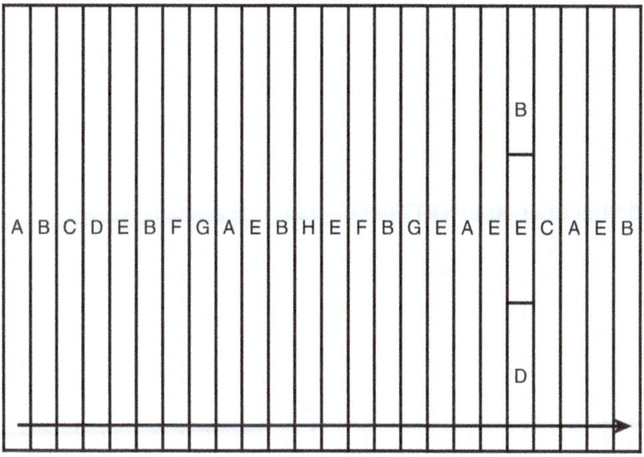

Figure 4.15 Character–storyline distribution in *Holiday Nightmare*

It looks chaotic at first sight. Some storylines seem pretty regular (the B and the E are the two major characters) but are the rest are too separate to work?

In fact, all storylines collide and are absorbed in the final third of the book. The reason they work initially in this fragmentary structure is because each contains an element of the other, either by direct reference or by featuring one of the other characters. The storylines are perspectival in the sense that each is seen through the eyes of a privileged character. Their view is limited – only the reader sees the bigger picture. We'll come back to this in more detail when we consider narrative perspective. On the following page we see the *Holiday Nightmare* diagram again (Figure 4.16), this time revealing which storyline elements of other chapters are referenced (in grey) within each fragment. What can you deduce from it?

Perhaps you saw that the A storyline is in some ways the unifying storyline – the one that references most other storylines (it features the most fragments of other stories within it). The A storyline is the village policeman who is investigating a number of different issues. The H storyline is the village priest who becomes inadvertently embroiled in most of the other issues and

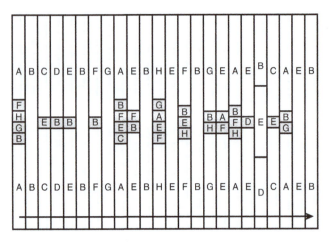

Figure 4.16 Inter-chapter storyline references in *Holiday Nightmare*

therefore becomes the main focus of the policeman's interest. The B storyline meanwhile, seems to pass obliviously through most of the first half. She's a foreigner who has no idea what's going on.

How exactly does each storyline feature in another? Usually in the most basic and unobtrusive way. In that first chapter, for example, the policeman receives a fax about two of the other storylines and hears personally from another character about another storyline. Often, the connection is nothing more than characters remarking on or observing events or characters in another storyline. They might meet inadvertently in a café. The story is set in a village and everyone sees everything.

The point is that this constant, albeit subtle, interplay between separate storylines keeps them all in the reader's mind at the same time. It's particularly emphatic in *Holiday Nightmare* because it has so many storylines. You might use it less in a story with fewer storylines. Compare it with the storyline diagram of *The Vice Society* that we saw above, this time with inter-chapter references added in grey (see Figure 4.17).

It's immediately clear that there are fewer storyline interconnectors here. The strongest pattern is of the two main characters

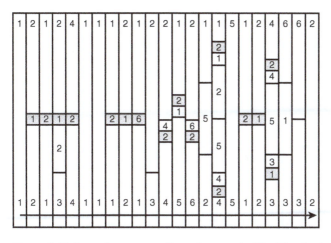

Figure 4.17 Inter-chapter storyline references in *The Vice Society*

constantly referring to, remembering or watching each other. As mentioned earlier, the stories meet about halfway through the book and spin out from there, each character taking a different strand of what has proved all along to be a single investigation.

The earlier point about the importance of beginning, middle and end has not been forgotten. So far, we've been considering how storylines are established and how they relate to each other as they develop. Theoretically, these storylines need never actually meet. They could exist independently of each other and offer pleasure merely by the subtle connections they suggest. This is something relatively rare, however, and could look like a literary exercise in narrative. It's much more common for storylines to meet at some point and lead to the satisfying conclusion of the novel.

When storylines do not combine, there is a curious effect whereby you get a staggered ending. Let's say you have three storylines set in different decades that do not actually combine into a singular thread. You'd have to have three separate endings: one for each storyline. One of them would be at the actual end of the book (the last page) while another might be three chapters back. Of, course, you could end all three with a paragraph each on the last page, but this takes you into the realms of expediency rather than reader pleasure. It's possible, but you can see the kinds of issues it raises.

Both *Holiday Nightmare* and *The Vice Society* see their multiple storylines coalescing in the final stretch, but a paradox presents itself here. A map of the last third of each book would NOT look busier or more complicated than the middle section. Why not?

Because there are not more storylines, characters or interconnectors. All of these have reached maximum number and complexity about 60 per cent into the plot. What makes the end of a novel satisfying is not an ever-increasing number of storylines (they might even be reduced), but an increase in other things: plot points, tension, pace, revelation and conclusions. They don't appear on the kind of diagrams we've seen above. We will see how they work below.

Single storylines

I said earlier that there are broadly two kinds of novel: the single storyline and the multiple storyline. Rationally speaking, the single storyline should be easier to plot. After all, it's pretty much just a straight line, right? Not quite.

The single storyline has to engage the reader in a different way. In the absence of multiple different threads, the single thread has to be given multiplicity and/or texture by other means. These could be:

- Different character perspectives
- Multiple occurrences
- Compelling character voices
- Pertinent digressions
- Stories within the story (could be flashback/backstory).

Moby Dick, for example, has a very simple plot. Its length and complexity come from the numerous episodes, the digressions about cetology and the experiences of the crew. These are not distinct storylines as such – they are merely facets of the main quest for the white whale. Ishmael, whose voice begins the book, has very little story of his own. He is rather Melville's mouthpiece and eyes on board the Pequod.

The essential requirement in the single storyline novel is that there is something for the reader to focus on. It might be a different thing on every page, or it might be broader movements like a symphony.

My novel *The Lost Archipelagos* was a single storyline novel of 200,000 words and fifty-three chapters. Though the storyline was quite complex in terms of plot twists, it was nevertheless just a journey from one place to another via numerous places in between. Texture was achieved using two of the above bullet points: different character perspectives and multiple occurrences. In other words, something new was always happening and a large group of people was experiencing them differently.

Below are two diagrams. The first is a rough representation (not by chapter) of where the ship sails. The second is a similarly rough view of some things (again, not by chapter) that happen along the way.

Despite the single storyline, you see that there's plenty to occupy the reader's attention. Each change of location is a new focus, each passage in between allows us to observe the passengers and crew on board, and each stage of the journey has numerous occurrences in which selected characters (or all of them) are challenged, amazed, entertained or put in jeopardy. As well as these things,

Cape Horn	(London)	Chile	Juan Fernandez	Easter Island	Pitcairn Island	Paumotu Islands	Tahiti	Marquesas Islands	Cook Islands	Kermadec Islands	Sydney, Australia	Loyalty Island	Fiji	Ellice Islands	Gilbert Islands	Nauru	Caroline Islands

Figure 4.18 Broad geographical divisions of *The Lost Archipelagos*

Storm – major characters introduced	(London – purpose for the voyage)	Slave trade – ship invasion – robbery – treasure	The Crusoes – murder in the caves	Native choir – attack – escape	The mutineers – insane governor – escape	The slaughter – clues	Colonial culture – the trial – more clues	Native orgy – the tattoo artist – escape	The robbed priest	The shipwrecked family – orgy	Committee meeting – revelations	Turtle hunt	Sea cucumber harvest – prisoners – cannibals	The ghost natives	Shark hunt – kidnap – moonblind	The robber king – prisoners – escape	Sea monsters	The castaways – the native brew	Intoxicated crew	Ship taken over	The treasure of de Fonte

Figure 4.19 Episodes in *The Lost Archipelagos*

there are also numerous character arcs, perspective changes and plot points within the storyline. A sample chapter might therefore have this kind of content:

- New location to explore (to interest the reader)
- A number of occurrences
- A number of new steps in the overall plot
- A number of character perspectives and/or arcs
- Dialogue (to manage pace)
- Description (to evoke atmosphere).

Lolita as a single storyline

As a conscious and wilful work of literature, *Lolita* has greater licence to digress and deviate from its central narrative thread. Nevertheless, the book must adhere to the same rules of storytelling coherence as any other book in order to be readable. That's why Nabokov is careful to seed the necessary story elements throughout, even if we don't realise until the end that he's done so. The character of Quilty is mentioned, or appears without name, at various points in the plot so that his eventual 'unmasking' does not come out of the blue. The reader has to acknowledge that all the clues were there.

The book also keeps us reading with joined episodic sections. The chapters set at Beardsley College represent a narrative frame of their own, as do the chapters travelling across country, the early backstory, and the 'three-year' montage later in the book. They are discrete pieces in an overall plot – joined by being part of a singular confession.

Above all, the book coheres as a single storyline because it's all framed within the context of a confession to a murder, which is made clear at the start. The main narrative line runs directly from that initial knowledge, through the progress of the various crimes, to the discovery of the murder victim. Whatever happens along the way, the destination has been specified.

By now, you'll have probably noticed that some other aspects of plotting have started to creep in without featuring in the diagrams. We've spoken about chronology and storylines, but these represent only part – a subtle and gradually revealed part – of what creates an engaging plot. We'll come to additional such elements in a moment, but first a quick look at a related point.

Stories within the storyline

The storylines we've been looking at so far all contain other stories within them. Most of those listed in the *Lost Archipelagos* diagram above could be extracted from the broader storyline and told just as they are. There's a chapter in *The Vice Society* in which Williamson and Noah visit a private asylum – another self-contained story within a broader storyline.

The point is always providing the reader with something to focus on – ideally a few things at the same time. Your role as author is to create a series of 'attention stepping stones' by which the reader moves through the novel. That is the focus of the next section.

Plot points and occurrence

Essentially, we're taking about what *happens* in the novel within the broader strands of storyline and character arc – the elements or episodes or scenes that incrementally and accumulatively make up the story itself. The plot points are the broad steps of the storyline, while occurrence might best be conceived as the steps between the steps – the small dots that connect the bigger dots. For example, a plot point sees our hero lose a finger in a bar fight, while the occurrence tells us how he gets into and out of the bar.

More than any other element of plot, these two are the ones that keep readers reading. The most sublime style, the greatest characters and the most brilliant idea will be wasted if nothing actually happens. The world of literature is noted for such books – the ones that everyone knows but nobody ever finishes. Genre fiction tends not to tolerate the empty plot.

True, the amount of plot points and occurrence depends on the kind of book you're writing. Certain genres tend to have more occurrence than actual storylines. The James Bond novels of Ian Fleming, for example, tend to have almost formulaic storylines (villain identified, villain pursued, Bond has a setback, Bond is challenged, Bond is triumphant) but derive their interest from the wonderful episodes that Fleming uses as building blocks for his story. (He also makes very effective use of research detail, educating his readers on such subjects as diamonds, gold, organised crime and heraldry.)

If a plot point is a necessary step in plot (discovery of a clue, revelation of a secret, kidnap of a nymphet), what constitutes an occurrence? It could be almost anything. Importantly, it need not always be directly connected to storyline. For example, the early chapters of *The Vice Society* see Mr Williamson working in mail fraud, though this has nothing whatsoever to do with the rest of the storylines. As well as being a way to introduce the reader to his proficiency as a detective, it also provides an interesting historical aside for the reader, sets the sociological scene and establishes an atmosphere in which nothing is as it seems. In *Moby Dick*, it might be a sub-scene in which Captain Ahab performs some pagan ritual with harpoon cups.

What constitutes an occurrence?

- A scene in which action is played out to some purpose
- A piece of dialogue
- A descriptive passage (towards some narrative purpose)
- A flashback or bit of backstory
- A digression on some subject
- A change in focus (location, character perspective)
- A 'set piece' episode
- A 'story within the story'.

I said earlier that my first novel was written according to a sort of 'shopping list' I'd drawn up regarding my own favourite elements in fiction. One of these was the 'set piece' episode: a big, brash and – above all – memorable scene that was timed to appear at a critical juncture in the plot and provide the reader with a really enjoyable experience. The successful set piece, I reasoned, was the kind of thing a reader would go back to read again and enjoy out of context. Evidently I succeeded in my aim. The first review of the book, in *The Guardian*, read:

The novel's spectacular set-pieces include a public hanging, a masked ball and a hot-air balloon chase. Well worth reading.
                                                            The Guardian (2009)

Plot points and occurrence are the stepping stones by which you lead the reader through your book. Storylines and character arcs take hundreds of pages to develop and resolve, so you need to be engaging the reader page after page with something else to grab their attention. It's not about just leaping maniacally from scene to scene, but rather thinking in terms of how you populate your character arcs and storylines with meaningful smaller pieces. Your occurrences have to move the story along, but they must also have meaning in their own right otherwise they'll seem arbitrary and disconnected.

For example, you wouldn't want to have your protagonist sit and read a newspaper for three pages merely because you need to bridge a narrative gap between his early arrival and his appointment at the dentist – unless something about that newspaper (and the narrative space given to it) is relevant to the character or the plot. Relevance is key. An occurrence makes the story move, but also adds a host of other things:

What else occurrence contributes

- Character-building
- Atmosphere/mood/tone
- Pace/action
- Metaphor/allegory
- Necessary knowledge
- Exploring theme
- Seeding motifs.

How much occurrence do you need?

Just enough to achieve your aims (assuming you know in advance what your aims are). Your story-building work should have given you a lot of material for possible scenes and storylines, which in turn should have suggested many possible plot points and occurrences. Things happen in connection with where you've come from in the plot and where you're going to. Basically, all occurrence is bridging work: the actual matter of narrative (dealt with below).

Occurrence is also essentially accumulative in the sense that it builds what the reader knows about the book, its world, its characters and its action. The more you reveal, the more they buy into the book, the greater the engagement. This doesn't mean suffocating with excessive occurrence.

As an example, let's look in detail at the fifteen-page prologue of *The Vice Society* (Table 4.1) and examine what it contains in terms of occurrence and intended effect.

Table 4.1 Occurrence and effect in *The Vice Society*

Occurrence	Intended effect
Woman plummets from the Monument.	Galvanising and grisly start to a novel with quite a dark subtext.
Woman's corpse described.	Playing on voyeuristic impulse in reader (another subtext) while also creating pathos.
Business of removing the body and putting it on public show. Husband arrives.	More pathos, and an introduction to what sort of society this is.
Jump to public inquest (reported as dialogue transcript).	Keep narrative going, using a dialogue-heavy technique to keep pace up and reveal numerous facts.
Different witnesses questioned by chairman.	Revealing the backstory to the actual fall and revealing subtle discrepancies/omissions that suggest it was in fact foul play.
Husband (Mr Williamson) appears to give evidence.	Increase pathos, up the stakes emotionally and lend depth to the scene.
His evidence contradicts the suicide impression.	Murder is suggested. Now all the evidence can be understood differently.
The verdict is given as suicide all the same.	A great injustice has occurred and must be righted. We'll come back to this later in the book.

Arguably, there are only really two main plot points in that prologue – the fall and the inquest – but I've listed all occurrences: the incremental steps by which you lead and direct the reader's attention throughout the plot. Indeed, it's commonly the case that one larger plot point will contain many smaller occurrences and this, as I said above, is narrative work (to be dealt with later). For example, in my third novel, the plot notes for one chapter read simply, 'Mr Newsome goes into the sewers'. That was the main plot point, but it took many more occurrences to get Mr Newsome there.

Though I talk about steps and points, it should be clear that no joins should be evident to the reader. There is only one break in this prologue: a double space to indicate lapsed time before the inquest. Since the two sections are so closely allied, it's not much of a stretch for the reader.

For comparison, Table 4.2 shows the first chapter of *The Lost Archipelagos*.

This occurs over twenty-two pages. Again, the only temporal break is before the switch of narrative perspective from omniscient to Mr Purvis. (We'll be looking at narrative perspective later.)

Table 4.2 Occurrence and effect in *The Lost Archipelagos*

Occurrence	Intended effect
A boat crew rows from shore to ship in thick fog.	A metaphor – the book is about being lost. Creates atmosphere and tone.
A whale swims close but unseen.	Another metaphor – threat is always hidden in the book. More tone and atmosphere.
The first mate goes to the captain's cabin. They discuss the trip round the Horn.	An introduction to both. Some minor backstory. Anticipation built for the Horn.
Captain called to meet his wealthy passengers. They discuss the trip round the Horn.	An introduction to the wealthy passengers. More anticipation.
The crew called on deck.	An introduction to them. More anticipation.
The ship steers out towards the Horn.	Pace picks up. The journey begins.
Character perspective and time shift: passenger Mr Purvis decides he wants to go up on deck.	Acclimatising reader to nature of polyphonic narrative to come and Mr Purvis' nature.
Mr Purvis emerges on deck in a raging tempest.	Action scene. Pace increasing.
Mysterious vessel glimpsed frozen into an iceberg. We leave it in peril.	Setting expectation for a novel of odd occurrences, strange characters and action.

The first two occurrences listed here occupy almost one page, but let's play devil's advocate and say they lasted for ten pages. If the reader picked the book up in a shop, I wonder if he would continue reading beyond three pages of atmospheric description. At some stage, the tacit question would occur: 'Fine – but what's actually happening?'

Literature is the exception. Cormac McCarthy's *Suttree* begins with four pages of intensely literary description in which nothing whatsoever happens. Much of the rest of the book is also apparently plotless description. How is such a book readable? Many online reviewers say it isn't, but this is some of the finest description you're ever likely to read in an English-language novel. It is absolutely sublime. We read on because we're amazed at the artistry.

This is not to say that those two occurrences in *Archipelagos* couldn't effectively be made to last ten pages if we wanted them to. One of the crew could be given a great speech like the iconic 'SS Indianapolis' monologue spoken by Quint in the movie *Jaws* – but there would have to be a reason for this. In this first chapter, the principal aim is to suck the reader in and get the story moving. Later, there is much more digression, but within established parameters of pace.

> *Don't say the old lady screamed – bring her on and let her scream.*
>
> Mark Twain (cited in Graham, 2014)

Distribution of plot points

We've considered how many plot points we might need, but we need also to consider how they're spread. A badly plotted novel will often see stretches where there is loads of occurrence (the end, the beginning) but then great wastelands where nothing much seems to happen.

There's nothing wrong, of course, with giving your story space to breathe and your plot points scope to develop.

Table 4.3 Plot points in *The Vice Society*

Chapter	Plot point
1	Newsome reveals facts of Holywell St death. Vice Society introduced.
2	Mr Williamson is working in mail fraud: his methods.
3	Holywell St described. Newsome and Cullen investigate.
4	Eusebius the Vice Society spy introduced – his secret mission.
5	Williamson's fraud investigation continues (suspect is the narrator).
6	Williamson goes to Monument and to cemetery. Receives letter about murder.
7	Williamson studies the letter and begins his investigation.
8	Mr Newsome's secret files – his ongoing investigation.
9	Williamson interrogates prostitute. Embarrassed. Contacts Noah.
10	Newsome and Cullen visit Poppleton's bookshop. Spy observes.

Sometimes the whole point is that nothing seems to be happening. Nevertheless, you need to remain in strict control of the distribution. If little is happening, make sure it's because you intended it, not because you couldn't think how to bridge a gap. Your plotting should show you where gaps may exist, and these should have been filled before you begin to write. At the very least, you should be aware that *something* is happening in each chapter or major fragment of your plot. Every piece should have a purpose that the reader can recognise as necessary and relevant.

Table 4.3 above shows a rough rundown of broad-stroke plot points in the first ten chapters of *The Vice Society* (after the prologue).

These are the big plot points – the reasons why the chapters exist as distinct pieces. They also contain many smaller occurrences I've not mentioned. As we've seen, both work alongside all the other material of plot: character arc, storyline and chronology, etc.

It's a very good idea, while at the plotting stage, to conceive your book as a simple diagram that looks something like this:

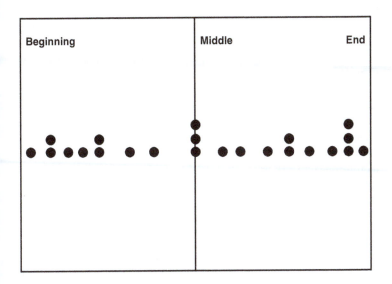

Figure 4.20 Example plot-point chart

The dots here represent major plot points, giving you an idea of when and where things should be happening and if you have enough going on in the novel. They might indicate chapters, or you might add chapter divisions later. If there are gaps, how do you intend to fill them? This also helps with chronology because you might decide to move plot points around depending on how the storylines play out. It's far, far easier to work out a plot in this way than by writing it all first and trying to move it later.

Engagement techniques

How do you decide the order of your storyline chronology? How do you decide when or how to introduce or dispose of a character?

How do you know where a chapter fits into the overall scheme? How do you know how long a chapter should be?

All of these questions amount to much the same thing: how do you ensure that the reader is feeling what you want them to feel when you want them to feel it? It sounds like manipulation – and that's exactly what it is! Writing as a writer means orchestrating your reader's experience. If a reader feels excitement, anticipation, fear, interest or shock, it should be because you engineered it. That's why we buy and read books – they are engineered experiences.

The trick – the art – of writing is identical to that of the master illusionist: to evoke a sense of wonder while hiding the mechanisms he calls 'magic'. It's a feat of concealment and it uses techniques like any other skill. We've already seen a few, but there are many more.

> *Reading is directed creation.*
>
> Jean-Paul Sartre (cited in Priest, 2002)

Some engagement techniques

- Great ideas and characters
- Good stories
- Storyline juxtaposition
- Chronological juxtaposition
- Set pieces
- Chapter length
- Suspense
- Twists and revelations
- 'Cliffhangers' and openers
- Conflict and pressure
- Pace.

Your novel can use all of these or some of them. Genre fiction tends to make use of some more readily, but it would be wrong to think that literary fiction doesn't. It just does so more subtly. Consider *Lolita*, in which there are two sections where Lolita is notably absent: in the backstory chapters where we anticipate her arrival, and in the period after her disappearance when Humbert searches for her. Both are examples of suspense. This stuff is the very essence of storytelling, whatever kind of novel you're writing.

Chapter length

This is something that most readers probably don't register as they read. At least, something is wrong if they do. It's certainly worth asking why chapters exist at all. Why do we need them? *Moby Dick* has 135. *Robinson Crusoe* hasn't got any.

Chapters provide distinct demarcations. They allow us to change focus, but that's hardly essential since we can do that mid-chapter as well. They also help the writer to structure a story, but again, most readers don't consciously stop after each chapter and acknowledge the structural element. They tend just to read on, drawn by the interplay of storylines or the single thread.

What chapters *do* accomplish is establishing a rhythm for the reader's experience of the book. They act at a subliminal level in setting tone and pace. The editor of my first book advised me to break one very long chapter into two more equal-sized ones for no other reason than that the reader had been acclimatised to a regular chapter-length by that point. If the chapter was longer, it might have seemed *unduly* long and therefore less interesting. In this sense, the chapter is like the actor's breathing: an unnoticed technique to promote fluency.

There's also the very practical courtesy of allowing your reader to fold a page and turn the light off. Paradoxically, many shorter chapters will encourage him to read further than one large chapter because he knows there's always an opportunity for a break. Your effective use of engagement techniques, however, ensures that each chapter break results in the decision for 'Just one more . . . '

Use your chapters wisely to manipulate the reader's psyche. Short chapters increase pace and keep the reader going. Regular mid-length chapters build a steady rhythm. A longer chapter tells the reader that this is a meaty episode (ideally one you've prefigured in the few chapters before it). In *Holiday Nightmare*, the longest chapter in the book is the final one, where all storylines come together in the climactic scene.

Kurt Vonnegut has written some books that appear to be a collection of disconnected paragraphs rather than chapters. The effect is curious: it sounds as if he's talking directly to the reader in his own voice and has chosen this structural form because it's nearest to verbal utterance. Tricky to pull off, but fantastic in the hands of this master.

Also remember to keep an eye on how the content of your chapters balances out over the whole plot. Two or three chapters of expositional detail will put the brakes on pace, while two or three of dialogue will speed it up. Always be aware of what's gone before and what is to follow. You may not notice this as you're writing, but a reader will definitely register it while reading.

Suspense

My dictionary offers such definitions as 'deferred', 'held back' and 'an atmosphere of nervous or excited uncertainty'. All imply the wilful withholding of an anticipated outcome.

It's not only crime novels that live and (let) die on their levels of suspense. Any good story should be asking the reader to anticipate, predict or fear future events in the story. It might simply be the end of the book, or it might be just one of many uncertainties you've planted into character arcs and storylines. The reader reads to *find out*. Books move forwards (even if they move backwards) and so the destination must always be desired.

The business of suspense is basically one of artful evasion, delay and disguise. The trick is to hint and suggest to the reader what the outcome *may* be – to create a sense of desire or dread. This can be done in a number of ways.

Creating suspense

- Make your characters want or seek something
- Make your characters fear or flee something
- Make some characters know what others do not
- Make the eventual pay-off a great prize or a terrible punishment
- Hide the objective truth in subjective perspectives
- Use chronology to hide missing pieces
- Make the storyline an investigation
- Give the reader what they want just a bit more slowly than they want it.

These are, admittedly, very broad descriptions. We've already seen how the interplay between storylines allows some characters to do and know things that other characters do not, and how prologues can pre-empt action. We've also seen how character types can play against each other and cause fireworks when they meet. Consider, too, how plot points can be tendentious, steering the reader towards an inevitable – but undefined – conclusion. The subject of character/narrative perspective is a question for later on, but let's look at some examples here.

In my novel *Holiday Nightmare*, I use an initial fragment to reveal two of the major plotlines: a secret nationalist cell that's been identified on the island, and an accusation of pagan sacrifices being carried out. The policeman must investigate both, immediately setting up expectation in the reader. Whatever else may happen, these two storylines must be followed and proved true or false. The policeman's job and reputation may depend on it. In the first fragment, a young girl is offered the opportunity of a lifetime to be the personal assistant to a Hollywood legend. She accepts, but there's something very dodgy about the deal. What will happen?

In *The Vice Society*, we see Inspector Newsome investigating an apparently innocuous fall from a window. But the more witness statements he collects, the more it becomes clear there's been a massive cover-up. It will take him the rest of the novel to sort through the clues towards a solution.

The Lost Archipelagos is not an investigation and so derives its suspense from other sources. These include: putting characters in jeopardy; having a 'secret storyline' that only one character knows; following storylines from multiple but partial perspectives so that the whole story comes from always reading on; and collecting clues in the search for a shipwrecked sailor. (In fact, there is also a section of the novel that does have a criminal investigation.)

As I've said, suspense is often associated with genre novels, particularly crime novels, yet many of my favourite literary novels supply notable examples of suspense mechanisms. *Lolita* begins with a foreword from a psychologist alluding to the protagonist's trial, and Humbert himself refers to himself as a murderer early on. We must read the whole book (pitched to us as a 'confession') to find out who gets murdered. Similarly, *Moby Dick* builds mystique around Captain Ahab from the outset, withholding his appearance until the Pequod is at sea and introducing a 'prophet' at the dock to prefigure the doomed voyage. We must read on to discover the truth.

It all comes down to promising something, predicting something, concealing something. This is hard to do if you're making it up as you go along. If you don't know what it is, how can you artfully conceal it from the reader (other than going back and rewriting a lot of the novel once you've found out)?

Twists and revelations

In complete opposition to suspense, the twist comes out of nowhere. Or at least that's how it seems – a good twist takes planning to pull off successfully. If it really does come out of nowhere, the reader won't buy it and it'll look like a cheap gimmick. Note how the character of Quilty is apparent, in one form or another, throughout *Lolita*.

The twist works because you've purposely lulled the reader into certain expectations concerning storyline and character. There has to be a foundation so that the amazement of the twist can still be rationalised as possible. And those storylines and characters must continue to work after the twist, so you need to know what the twist has changed and what it hasn't. Essentially, you're writing two storylines: the one that the reader knows about and the one you're going to switch to. The twist is the bridge or the pivot.

Twists normally come at the end because that's where they have the most impact. The twist in Ian McEwan's *Atonement* is perhaps the most famous of recent years. This is not to say, however, that you can't use more than one and at different stages of your novel.

The Lost Archipelagos was very long, with the mid-point landing around the 100,000-word mark. For this reason, I dropped a big twist in the middle. It re-contextualised everything that had happened and re-set the stakes for the rest, thus re-energising a very long storyline. There was also another twist at the end.

Revelation is something slightly different and could fall under the definition of a major plot point. Like a twist, it changes the way the reader engages with and understands the plot, but it doesn't necessarily reverse or rewrite the action. A revelation is also slightly easier to pull off because you can drop it into the storyline like a bomb and watch the reaction. Raymond Chandler once wrote that if he didn't know what was going to happen next, he'd have a man walk in into the room holding a gun.

Revelations can act as much-needed pulse beats and you might – depending on the type of novel – choose to time them so that they appear reasonably regularly. You can also withhold them, and keep threatening to drop them. In *Holiday Nightmare*, one of my characters had a secret that only he and the reader knew. Revelation of it would cause an apocalyptic reaction, and so I enjoyed putting him in situations where it was always threatening to come out. In this case, a twist saved him from the worst of it.

'Cliffhangers' and openers

'Cliffhangers' are reminiscent of those 1950s TV serials where the hero was literally left hanging off a cliff at the end of the episode. Such a gambit would not be terribly subtle in a novel, but that doesn't mean the technique isn't usable in other forms.

It's helpful to think of a chapter as a microcosm of the novel. Everything is encoded within it (storyline, character, location, themes, etc.). So if a novel derives its momentum from structure, so should the chapter itself. One way of maximising the effect is by using cliffhangers – not necessarily the 'bus hanging over the precipice' kind of thing, but a revelation, or phrase, or occurrence that acts as structural punctuation in the overall storyline. It should be something that underlines what went before, that cues up an event to come, or which acts as a pivot between storylines.

The function of the cliffhanger is partly connective, partly divisive. It connects to sections that will come but provides a decisive break with what's just happened. It's a curious phenomenon that the end of a chapter is better remembered than its beginning or middle, and so a good cliffhanger leaves the reader in no doubt that the chapter they've just read was instrumental to the plot. If they learned one thing, it was the last thing mentioned.

By the same token, chapter beginnings (or openers) are important because they often follow a cliffhanger. If you've just left the reader's mind echoing with the gong of a cliffhanger revelation, you have to snatch back their attention with the first lines of the next chapter. This is especially true if you're using multiple storylines and need to move the reader smoothly between them. It's necessary to suck the reader back into a thread they last saw two chapters previously (and which may have ended with its own cliffhanger).

The kind of opener you choose naturally depends on the effect you want to achieve. Dialogue is a good way of dropping a reader straight into a fresh storyline, whereas a long piece of description might act as a necessary brake on the pace as you lead the reader into some complex expositional stuff. We'll consider this kind of thing later when we think about pace.

Table 4.4 on the following page shows some examples of openers and cliffhangers in *The Vice Society*. These are the kinds of things you'd typically find in a thriller. Literature tends to disdain such techniques as rather crass and obvious. They needn't be. A chapter can end just as effectively with a mordant line

Table 4.4 Openers and cliffhangers in *The Vice Society*

Chapter	Opener	'Cliffhanger'
1	Boss to Newsome: 'Tell me everything.'	Boss to Newsome: 'Go there now.'
2	Descriptive riff: two-faced London.	Narrator first revealed: 'It was I.'
3	Descriptive riff: Holywell Street.	Newsome: 'Let's go out into the alley.'
4	Who had been that man listening at the door?	'Well, be on your way.'
5	Scullery maid: 'What d'yer want?'	Williamson: 'The villain is close.'
6	The villain in coffee house.	Letter: 'Your wife was murdered.'
7	Williamson examines the letter.	A spy has seen everything.
8	Who was the lurking observer?	Cullen soon to be working with Williamson.
9	Williamson strolls to prostitute's flat	Williamson contacts Noah Dyson

of dialogue, an allegorical description, a lament for lost time, a vague or ambiguous fade-out. You use them as appropriate. You might think the following cliffhangers are from Raymond Chandler: *(Drew his .32 automatic, I guess, and put a bullet through his moll's eye)... 'First time I've seen a man in a smoking jacket, sir – except in movies, of course'... To myself I whispered that I still had my gun, and was still a free man – free to trace the fugitive, free to destroy my brother.* They are all from *Lolita*.

A word of warning, though. Take care to monitor how you begin and end each chapter. It's too easy to fall into a pattern that becomes repetitive and therefore predictable to the reader. If this happens, you lose the effect. The answer is to use a variety of techniques: description, dialogue, character perspectives, plot points etc. so that the reader never knows what's coming.

Conflict and pressure

Have you ever seen a classic disaster movie from the 1970s or 1980s? A plane loses its instruments and flies towards a volcano. A plane crash-lands in the mountains. A ship rolls over and the passengers are caught inside. The hero must lead a group of survivors to safety and this group usually consists of a familiar set of types: a rival alpha male, a dumb and busty love interest, a honeymooning couple (one of whom always dies), a priest or nun whose faith is challenged, and a philosophical elderly one whose death teaches us a lesson. More importantly, there's always a 'difficult' one whose action jeopardises survival for everyone. They're weak, complaining, cowardly and usually treacherous in some way. Naturally, they inevitably die in some spectacularly satisfying manner. This person represents conflict.

Conflict is what prevents or delays the thing you want to happen. It's the character who works against the hero, the fog bank that prevents the essential take-off, the kidnapping that ruins the honeymoon, the captain asking for your badge and gun. It's another candidate for the term 'plot point' and a key engagement technique.

Kurt Vonnegut said that your character should always want something, even if it's just a glass of water. Suspense dictates that he or she first gets thirsty. Conflict dictates that someone else drinks the water first. (And the twist reveals it was vodka all along.)

Conflict prolongs action, thus aiding suspense. It creates empathy for those it affects and antipathy towards those who create it. In my own books, Inspector Newsome was created explicitly as a catalyst for conflict. He is smart, calculating, ambitious and unscrupulous, which means he often has the upper hand over his competitor: the fair-minded and ethical Mr Williamson. The only way to beat Newsome is to be smarter (or more calculating, more ambitious, more unscrupulous), which is why Mr Williamson usually ends up going to Noah Dyson. There's a scene in *The Vice Society* where Newsome happily drops Noah into peril and then runs off, causing the reader to hate him and to root even more strongly for Williamson.

In *Lolita*, Humbert has to marry Lolita's mother to get to Lolita, and then get rid of the mother when she finds out about his sordid tastes. Then Humbert has to identify and track the man he thinks is trying to rob him of his stepdaughter. It's all conflict.

Pressure is something different. Indeed, it's almost the opposite. If conflict prevents, pressure compels. Classic examples include the police captain who gives his detective twenty-four hours to solve the case, or the kidnap victim who has only ten hours of air, or the bomb on the bus that explodes if it goes below a certain speed. The reader may want something to happen (the pressure of the happy ending in romance) or fear it happening (the time bomb reaching zero).

Pressure is that nagging impetus that should always be in the reader's mind as they move through the storylines. It is one of their reasons for reading on. What if the hero doesn't make it in time? What if that secret is revealed? What if she says no? What if the deduction was wrong? There's also pressure in the use of dramatic irony: when the reader, or a character, knows something that others don't know and every event is charged with that lack of knowledge. The most famous example must be Oedipus marrying his mother and bringing divine retribution on Thebes. He searches for the culprit and discovers it's himself.

While plotting, it's therefore good to think about what might stand in the way and what might compel events to happen or not happen. What barriers can you erect for your characters? What traps can you prepare for them? How can you make the reader feel for the good guys, hate the bad guys and yearn for a resolution? It's a universal trope of storytelling that there *has to be something at stake* – a reason to read on. Without the uncertainty of pressure and the frustration of conflict, everything is a foregone conclusion.

Table 4.5 Conflict and pressure techniques

Ways with conflict	Ways with pressure
The recalcitrant character, the rival	Time constraints
The barrier to progress	Expectation
The struggle with the self	The need for happy resolution
The unknown	Hidden truth – when will it come out?
Actual violence	Dramatic irony

Pace

Some books move quickly; some move slowly. All should move at some pace, ideally varying according to the nature of the storyline. Along with all the other things we've discussed as part of engagement, pace works to manipulate the reader experience.

Pace sometimes gets a bad name. It's often associated with genre novels, particularly thrillers, and comes with the assumed taint of the 'page-turner' – the disposable holiday read or the ephemeral bestseller. Such associations generally relate to books that move at breakneck speed from start to finish, while conveniently forgetting that the opposite proposition is no more appealing. A slow and turgid novel earns no kudos for its lack of pace.

Engagement comes through the variation in pace: in marrying the speed of the narrative to the action it describes. You decide how fast or slowly the reader reads by engineering the prose in such a way that he has no choice but to accede. The techniques are not difficult, but they can be used subtly and artfully if required.

The last entry is perhaps a little contentious. There's no reason why a single storyline can't move quickly if given enough plotting, but a slowly paced multiple-storyline novel is at risk of inducing narcolepsy in the reader, particularly if it's narrated omnisciently.

Table 4.6 Pacing techniques

Slowing the pace	Raising the pace
Digression and explication	Multiple plot points and occurrence
Interior monologue	Dialogue
Long paragraphs	Short paragraphs
Long chapters	Short chapters
Limited perspectives	Multiple, changing perspectives
Subtle (or no) cliffhangers and openers	Provocative cliffhangers and openers
Evocative description	Spare description
Single storyline	Multiple storylines

Storyline interplay demands a certain amount of change to remain interesting and cohesive.

As with plot points, it can be very helpful to get an aerial view of your novel in terms of pace. When should it be fast? When should it be slow? Whatever the pace is doing, you need to be in control of it. Create a diagram at the plotting stage:

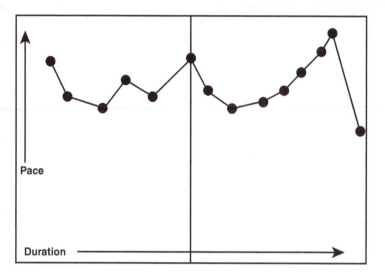

Figure 4.21 Example pace chart

This is not a real novel pace map, but you get the idea. Moving between plot points, we begin on a relative high to hook the reader, relax a bit to establish characters and storylines, rise to a catalyst, perhaps add a bit more context, and then spike the storylines in the middle. It all seems to go a bit dull after that, but rises gradually to the climax before settling down into a post-finale round-up.

If you have a diagram like this to hand as you work on storylines, there's no reason why your novel should have any tedious dry patches or gaps where not much seems to happen. It could prove critical in a thriller, and certainly important in a more cerebral work.

Subplots

Real life often seems to be more about subplots than plots. There are numerous stories, but few connections. That's why subplots in novels help to add texture. They act as echoes to the main action and give a sense of fullness to the overall structure. As with incidental characters, the absence of expectation around them also offers scope for some fun.

What's a subplot? It's basically a fragmentary storyline that runs underneath or alongside the main storylines – fragmentary, because it doesn't have the same requirement for development and resolution. It works as an adjunct rather than as an entity. When it pops up, the reader recognises it and draws some pleasing parallel with the main action.

A subplot is by no means essential. Sometimes, however, you develop a fondness for a particular character or theme or location and want to give it more room on the stage. If you find it sufficiently interesting to flesh out, the reader probably will, too. As long as the subplot doesn't begin to overshadow or distract from the main storylines, it will be an extra pleasure.

An example. My series of Victorian thrillers features a secondary character called Mr Cullen: a junior policeman who, in the first book, gets embroiled in a major case alongside his hero Mr Williamson. Cullen is a bit dim, but is earnest and loyal. In *The Vice Society*, he has his dream realised when he's seconded into the Detective Force alongside Inspector Newsome and we follow his uneven progress throughout the book. He doesn't have his own storyline. Rather, he tags along with the major characters and we occasionally see the action through his eyes. Like the classical Greek chorus, he allows us to glimpse the big picture from the common man's perspective. The awe in which he holds Williamson and Noah makes them seem greater and he more human.

Another example. In *Holiday Nightmare*, numerous references are made to the screenwriter of the movie that's being shot in the novel. However, this screenwriter does not feature in any of the storylines and never once appears in person. All we know of him is revealed in the occasional throwaway comments of other characters, and a story emerges that's utterly ludicrous. After some time, the reader is semi-consciously expecting the next ridiculous instalment. It's nothing more than texture, but pleasurable all the same.

The value of the subplot is largely derived from its seeming irrelevance and disposable nature. Like real life, it provides a quirky, surprising counterpoint. As John Lennon said: 'Life is what happens when you're busy making other plans.'

Themes and motifs

Perhaps your original idea was a theme, or perhaps the story-building stage suggested a few to play with. Themes are very useful structural elements because they provide guidance in terms of storylines. Very often while plotting my books, I'll go back to the theme and consider how the next scene or chapter might explore another aspect of it. The theme runs beneath everything that happens, even if it doesn't always appear visible to the reader.

Anthony Burgess complained that reviewers and readers failed to spot many of his subtleties with theme or structure, particularly the way he used music as an influence. I'm not sure it's strictly necessary. If the reader gets it, that's great; if not, it's arguably more important that the theme helped the writer to structure a coherent plot.

My first book grew out of an interest in observation and identity in the Victorian city. This in turn led me to create characters and scenes that could examine the various thematic facets that interested me. Thus, we had the members of a travelling freak show (always under scrutiny), a character who wore disguises (changing his identity at will), a mute (whose history had to be guessed) and many scenes that involved unusual perspectives: a public hanging, a masque and a balloon trip above the city. Perhaps most readers never made the connection, but the theme proved invaluable for me in tying the storylines together.

Holiday Nightmare grew out of an experience, but my research offered me the theme of reality and how we present it. Hollywood reality is not the same as our real lives. The portrayal of Greece as a tourist destination is not the same as the country itself. Even the way we portray ourselves is not always the same as our secret selves. This loose theme proved very handy in characterisation and in guiding how certain scenes played out. For example, an actor in the novel has literally lost any sense of the difference between his real life and life before the camera.

A theme can be mapped just as a story can. How many permutations and variations can you think of? How deeply do you want to explore your theme? A literary novel might expend more energy on this than on story, creating one of those books about which we say something like: 'Oh. It's about man who goes off to catch a fish – but what's it's *really* about is . . . ' Here, of course we're into the realms of allegory. Think about William Golding's *Lord of the Flies*, in which a group of boys marooned on an island becomes an allegory of human civilisation itself, each of the boys representing facets such as rationality, religion and aggression. Such patterns are highly engaging as the reader slowly pieces them together.

Some might argue the finer points of what separates a motif from a theme. By 'motif', I'm thinking of a device in the novel that exemplifies, represents or otherwise illustrates the theme or an element of it. It might be a character, a word or an object. In Vladimir Nabokov's *The Defence* (about a chess grandmaster who goes insane), it is the black and white chequerboard pattern that the character seems to see everywhere and which acts as a symbol of his life's limited moves. In Norman Mailer's *An American Dream*, the sexual act is a motif whose changing form throughout the book reflects the different aspects of the American Dream. Other novels have made use of the language of flowers, or figures from mythology, or colours. *Lolita* offers us the tantalising motif of a grubby overweight man glimpsed through windows or in the background: the author himself revealed through a slit in the narrative curtain? (In his *Lectures on Literature*, Nabokov notes the same motif in Joyce's *Ulysses*.)

Again, there will be readers who never notice these things, but this needn't stop you using them as constructive elements – as punctuation to your themes. It helps to know that you'll be using your motif in chapters four, seventeen and twenty-two.

Chapter checklist

It should be clear by now that the chapters (or fragments, or whatever you choose to call the separate 'chunks' of your novel) are the combinative elements of the structure. How they accumulate and interact is how your novel functions as an organic entity. As such, they provide a fabulous opportunity to help the author plan a plot in advance.

Each chapter is essentially a microcosm of the novel. It contains characters, plot points, occurrence, themes, subplots, etc. and it should be perfect in its own right. In planning any novel, you should be clear before you begin what you're going to put in each chapter. This way, you'll be able to see clearly and at a glance where gaps may lurk or where the story unravels. Prepare a chapter checklist and you'll see the DNA of your novel before you write a word.

It's up to you whether you do this as a rough mental plan or as a formal written table. Table 4.7 on the following page shows the kinds of things you should have on your chapter checklist, alongside examples from *The Vice Society*.

Such a checklist for every chapter will provide you with a bullet-proof plot with which to begin writing. But not yet! There are a few more essential considerations before you start to type . . .

The textured plot checklist

The aim of the structuring exercise is to create an immersive reading experience: seamlessly combining a number of different characters and storylines into a framework that's given dimension and texture by its detail, themes and narrative drive. The reader is engaged at every point by a number of complementary elements, all of which provide satisfaction.

Table 4.7 Chapter checklist from *The Vice Society*

Chapter element	Chapter 1 from The Vice Society
Characters featuring	Mr Williamson. Ambiguous reference to 'other men' as villains.
Character arc	Establishing W as tragically wronged figure.
Storyline	This crime is an early experiment by a corrupt perverts' club.
Plot points	Victim falls from Monument. Evidence suggests foul play.
Occurrence	The fall. The reaction. The inquest. The evidence. The wrong verdict.
Relation to other chapters?	Prefigures and reinforces revelation at end of Chapter 6
Themes	Revenge. Corruption at high levels. Public thirst for the lurid.
Motifs	Falling as a physical and moral concept
Subplot	N/A
Cliffhanger	Narrator reveals all of this will be important later . . .
Opener	Woman in mid-air, falling . . .
Chronology	Seven years before main action.
Pace	Urgent, to hook reader before four expository chapters
Research notes	Material from *Times* Archive re. genuine Monument suicides/inquests.
Other notes	Replicate the inquest with same typography/layout as in *The Times*

It's like watching a film at the cinema. In any one frame, you're following a character in a location in a plot. But you're also listening to a soundtrack, perceiving extras in the background, juggling perceptions created by editing and being subliminally affected by a colour palette, the cinematographer's framing and the tone of a particular film stock. This is texture. If the same shot were simply an actor reading lines from a sheet against a white background, it wouldn't have quite the same effect.

At any point in your plotting and structuring, you should be aware of such things as:

- Where are we in the overall plot?
- Where are we in this particular storyline?
- Where are we in this character's arc?
- How do other storylines play against this moment?
- How do other characters fit in with what's happening now?
- What's the background context (location, tone)?
- What's happening with pace?
- What's happening with theme?
- What's the immediate focus (occurrence)?
- What's coming next?
- What's the reader's stake at present?
- What should the reader be feeling right now?

Remember: plot is no more than footprints left in the snow after your characters have run by on their way to incredible destinations.

Ray Bradbury (2015)

Structure in summary

- Understand the difference between story, plot and narrative.
- Think about the projected length of your book.
- Is your novel of a particular type?
- Can you identify a beginning, middle and end in your idea?
- Think first in terms of broad structural elements.
- What chronology do you expect to use in your novel?
- Think about character mix and character arcs.
- Are you working with multiple or singular storylines?
- How do you arrange elements of a multiple storyline?
- Have you got enough content for a single storyline?
- What are your plot points/occurrences?
- How are they distributed?
- Have you considered pace (from the reader's point of view)?
- Are you using engagement techniques effectively?
- Do you have subplots? How do they fit in?
- How do themes and motifs work through the plot?
- What narrative approach are you taking?

Plotting exercises

- Try to conceive your story as numbered steps from start to finish. Plot it on paper and spend some time thinking about any additional steps (or other stories) you might intersperse. Do the same for books other people have written. It's very useful to get a visual/spatial representation of the story.

- Set yourself the task of writing some sample episodes from your projected story but at different lengths: 500, 1,000, 1,500 words. What feels most natural to you? This will help you gauge word count.

- Try to find a pre-existing model for your intended novel structure and use it as a pattern to help build your framework. It might be episodic like *The Odyssey*, a quest like Umberto Eco's *Baudolino*, an investigation, or a revenge story like Martin Amis's *The Information,* etc. Do a breakdown of the chapters and figure out how the book works. This isn't cheating. It's learning.

- Go back to one of your favourite books and read it again (as a writer) in terms of a single character arc. Make notes of the key stages of that character's development from start to finish and try to map it in terms of highs/lows or lessons learned. How do other characters help this single character to develop? How consistently and frequently do the stages occur?

- Pick up a book you've already read (or watch a film) and try to determine if anything significant happens around the mid-point. How about 20 per cent from the start or 20 per cent from the end? If you plotted the major occurrences of the book on a beginning–middle–end frame, where would they fall in terms of page numbers?

- Draw a line representing the chronological movements of a novel you know well. Where does it look backwards or forwards? Where does time speed up or slow down?

Try to collect a variety of such lines so you can see at a glance how novel chronology can work.

- Draw a spider diagram of characters in your work or someone else's. How do characters connect, reflect and act for or against each other? Shakespeare plays are a very good place to begin because every character has a necessary role. Sort these characters into lists of primary, secondary, tertiary depending on their importance in the storylines.

- Watch a commercial Hollywood film and keep a note of what happens according to the running time, i.e. boss lays out the challenge (5–7 mins from the start), car chase (10–15 mins from the start), meets new partner (15–20 mins from the start). You'll soon begin to see that certain scenes exist purely for the sake of pace, usually interspersed with necessary story elements.

- Read a literary novel and try to identify some of the engagement techniques mentioned in this chapter. Is there tension, suspense, pressure? If there are no apparent techniques, what makes the novel readable?

- Read a 'plotless' novel (see the 'Thematic reading list') and try to figure out what makes it readable – if it *is* readable.

- Try writing your first page – or a character scene – from a few different narrative perspectives (past/present, first- or third-person) and see what feels most natural.

5   Narrative approaches

I said earlier that narrative is how plot relates story. This involves occurrence (what's actually happening) but also a number of other, more subtle, elements that strongly affect the reader's engagement with the novel. More precisely, narrative is the lens through which the reader is compelled to see (or not see) the action. From what standpoint do they experience it? Through the character's eyes? Through the character's mind? As a scene unfolding cinematically? With the benefit of informed retrospect? The chosen perspective flavours the reader's experience and so tells them what to think, how to feel and, ultimately, how to read.

Compare the following extracts and note what a difference the narrative approach makes to how you see the action:

1   *I walked into the bar and looked around. I didn't see Jack. The barman asked me what I'd have and I told him my usual. He gave me a mojito with an umbrella in it.*

2   *I walk into the bar and look around. I don't see Jack. The barman asks me what I'm having and I tell him my usual. He gives me a mojito with an umbrella in it.*

3   *I walk into the bar. Scan the place. No Jack. 'What're ya havin'?' says the barman. 'The usual.' A mojito with umbrella. Looks good.*

4   *The bar was empty. Goddammit, Jack! Might as well get a drink. The usual: mojito with a brolly.*

5   *Jeff walked into the bar and looked around. He didn't see Jack. The barman asked him what he'd have and Jeff told him the usual. The barman gave him a mojito with an umbrella in it.*

6   *You go into bar and look around. You don't see Jack. The barman asks you what you're having and you tell him the usual. He gives you a mojito with an umbrella in it.*

7   *Jeff burst into the bar and looked wildly around. Jack wasn't there, so Jeff mooched to the bar. 'What'll you have?' said the barman, grinning. Jeff laconically ordered his usual: a mojito with an umbrella.*

8   *Jeff walked into the bar and looked around. No Jack. He went to the barman. 'What'll you have?' said the barman. 'The usual?' Why not? The barman handed him the mojito with an umbrella.*

Each one relates pretty much the same information, but with a very different feel. In each case, the narrative style has manipulated the reader not only into a way of seeing but of *inhabiting* the text to varying degrees.

Narrative style positions the reader by concealing or revealing, by dictating perspective and by setting mood. Why does the second seem more immediate, more literary, than the first? Why does the fourth seem edgier and more gripping than the fifth? Why does the seventh seem somehow false and contrived?

These are the parameters you need to be considering before you write your book. They dictate the path your reader will take into the plot you've designed and the amount of engagement they experience inside that plot. Too many writers don't consider such things, or consider them only partially, so that the eventual novel feels schizophrenic in its presentation of events. It's your responsibility as the writer to set the tone, create the atmosphere and the world of your text, and maintain it without flaw or contradiction. An inconsistent narrative style is like a fake accent – once you start to hear the dodgy vowels, it's game over. The illusion is broken.

There are advantages and disadvantages to every narrative approach. Some of the narrative approaches we might look at are:

- Authorial perspective and voice
- Character perspective and voice
- Subject address (person)
- Tense.

Authorial perspective and voice

How visible are you as the author of your own work? Are you the orchestrating, omniscient voice telling the reader what's happening? Naturally, *all* narrative is the author speaking, but there are levels of invisibility. Examples five, seven and eight above are the obvious authorial perspectives, in which the controlling voice recounts the details for the reader.

Even here, though, there are clear differences. Sentence five above takes care to maintain narrative distance, telling us only what we need to know to see the scene. Extraneous comments or colouring are left out, thus making the scene more cinematic. Sentence seven sees the author making more of an appearance in the many distinctive verbs and adverbs. This is the writer showing off their writing (their voice) – a bad thing when the writing is this amateurish, because it puts the writer between the reader and the action. It can be a good thing, however, when the writer's style is something special. Will Self appears to be one of those novelists whose style arguably comes through more strongly than the world of his books. His language stands between him and the objective world of his subject (what Anthony Burgess called 'opaque style') but his readers value the books for just this reason.

Sentence eight seems to straddle two camps. There's obviously an author at work here (telling us about Jeff) but there are also Jeff's own thoughts interposed ('free indirect speech' for those who like lit-crit terminology). This can be a tricky one to pull off for first-time novelists because the balance has to remain discreet and consistent between author and character. It takes practice to get it right and, as with a slipping foreign accent, a reader will pick up on the slightest discrepancies. On the other hand, it's a great way to have the best of both worlds, combining character and author perspective.

Character perspective and voice

All the other sentences above (apart from five, seven and eight) offer a distinct character perspective and, again, the differences are subtle but persuasive. Following a character puts us right inside the story, seeing it from their point of view. It could be one character or many. The trick is to ensure that the character in question is evoked in as realistic and convincing a manner as possible. If we're going to follow them and be asked to empathise, we need to feel that they're real and that their motivations are rational within the parameters of who they are. It's even more the case with multiple characters, because there must be discernible differences in voice and attitude. (This is arguably the same with an authorial view of characters, but it's certainly more important when we're given someone's eyes and ears.)

Sentences four and six are interesting in the degree to which they push identification. Four makes no sort of pretence at introducing or providing intercession for the character's voice. We're just right inside Jeff's head hearing his thoughts. It's a powerful technique, but could become very claustrophobic for the reader. It might be used with serial killers or madmen to evoke their unbalanced state of mind.

Sentence six uses the notoriously unpopular second-person address, in which the reader is asked to put themselves in exactly the same shoes. 'You' is essentially the reader. It's unpopular because it robs the reader of their independence and presumes that they will side with the second-person character (who is often a bit weird anyway). It's wearing and presumptuous, but it can work in small amounts if used alongside first person.

My novel *Holiday Nightmare* has eight storylines told through alternating short fragments. What would be the best narrative approach for such a book? I settled on an omniscient narrator with pertinent lapses into free indirect voice for the major characters only. Because most of the characters mix with other characters in their fragments, it was necessary to choose a dominant character perspective for each fragment and narrate from that character's point of view. Thus, the policeman in the story is referred to as 'Nikos' in his own fragments but as 'the policeman' or 'Sergeant Petras' or 'Petras' in the fragments of other characters. Accordingly, we're able to see into his thoughts only in his chapters. Here are two examples:

Character's own fragment

Nikos sighed and looked at his watch. He anticipated Maria's fury. Car trouble – that was probably the best excuse. He took a blunt pencil from the desk and was about to go down to let the air out of a tyre when the fax machine below the notice-board began to whine and chug.

Other character's fragment

The policeman studied him quite casually, seeming to assess his footwear, his clothing, his build and his general level of grooming. All the while, the policeman's moustache twitched in apparent amusement.

Subject address (person)

One of the first choices you have to make before you start writing is how you pitch a character's perspective. Look again at extracts one and five. They're identical apart from the form of address, but you can immediately see that the first brings you closer to the action whereas the other distances you from it.

Whatever choice you make, you will have to weigh the various pros and cons against what you want to achieve in your novel. Depending on your approach, some of the cons might also seem pro:

This is a simplistic breakdown. With some subtlety, there's no reason why all of them might not be used in some combination or other. For example, you might have a first-person narrator who (for chronological reasons) is able to stand outside the plot and narrate other people's stories in retrospect. You might have a first-person narrator who occasionally addresses the reader, cosying up to them with an overfamiliar or unhinged tone. You might opt for an omniscient third-person narrator who utilises free indirect speech to the extent that first-person creeps in. Here are some examples of those:

I'd missed the bus, but Darren hadn't. He'd been at home sniffing glue with his mates and watching Animal Hospital. *That's when his cousin had arrived with the stolen PC.*

I've always hated rabbits. Something about that sniffing thing they do, you know? You know when you're feeding them a bit of lettuce and they do that sniffing thing?

Jake opened the box. He peered inside. Empty. Nothing. Where was the money? Where was the letter? What was Johnny going to do now? I'm dead.

Table 5.1 Subject address comparison

Address	Pros	Cons
First (I)	Greater intimacy/connection	Other characters seen only by 'I'
	Privileged, idiosyncratic viewpoint	Limited viewpoints/knowledge
	Possibly more dynamic	Danger of lapsing into biography
Second (you)	Evokes 'unhinged'	Evokes 'unhinged'
	Emphasises first person	Presumes reader's complicity
Third (he/she)	Allows more perspectives	Distances reader more than first (I)
	Character expressed by behaviour	Danger of revealing authorial self

Narrative approach makes such a huge difference to how your novel affects the reader. It might also stamp a label on your novel as a commercial proposition. If you're using combined narrative approaches in quite a sophisticated way, it's usually because your book and its subject are aimed at a particular market sector or readership. Your average pulp-thriller reader might balk at too much free indirect speech, just as your literature lover might tire of an apparently simple first person. One is too complex, the other not complex enough.

Again, there are exceptions. Charles Bukowski's first-person narrator, Henry Chinaski, uses language so simple it might almost be a children's book, but he is often describing a life of alcoholic hopelessness and abuse. The one lesson is this: choose your narrative approach carefully to suit your novel.

Tense

There are at least twelve tenses in the English language, but we'll settle on two for the sake of simplicity (and because most of those twelve are variations on the basic past, present and future).

Extracts one and two above are identical but for the tense. The effect is quite similar to the first/third person difference in that present tense adds a certain tension and immediacy. You're right there with the character, not looking back. Present-tense narration is a technique much loved by literary fiction and for this reason it tends to be overused by first-time novelists who believe that it adds a literary gloss to their writing. I'm not a fan. It seems an affectation to me, and one that rapidly loses its impact after the reader becomes acclimatised to it (as he does to whatever narrative approach you adopt).

Changing tense throughout the book can have some advantages. You might use past/present to differentiate characters or chronological storylines. It's also quite nice to lapse from past tense into present when you want to quicken pace and emphasise immediacy:

> *They ran through the midnight alleys, their boots clattering and sparking on cobbles. The dogs pursued silently. A trip. A fall. John rolls. The dogs catch up. His scream echoes through the darkness.*

In *Lolita*, Nabokov writes Chapter 11 (Part One) in present tense while the rest of the novel is in past tense. This is because (ostensibly) he's quoting from a journal written at the time. From a purely authorial-narrative point of view, however, he's chosen present tense to evoke the febrile immediacy of his initial lust for Lolita.

Narrative and occurrence

There are different levels of plotting. Some people are happy with a rough list of chapters and their content, a clutch of storylines and a good sense of how they're going to play out over a specified word count. That's really the focus and the extent of this book. The onus thereafter is on the writing itself. As an indication, here is a verbatim snippet of some original plot notes for three chapters of *Holiday Nightmare* (typos included):

> *JIM – more problems with tourists. Accident? Forced to lead an excursion when excursion leader has ludicrous accident. the Greek night in all its horror. catalogue of tourists.*
>
> *PHILLIPA??goes back to village and diog bar – meets Grace there and talks to her properly about film, their ambitions. a spark. her concerns about star and script. he agrees to help . . . his admission. star not dead, but missing. she's mad – he has to tell police. press sniffing around? Problems with hotels/tourists. Has spoken to police. Welcome meeting – secret tourist present?*
>
> *GRACE – rewrites name of film changed. Got to make it work without reshooting. Got to pacify star. it's all becoming a farce. Chet wnats a piece of it. Where's CAro? Not in Trailer. Not in Villa. gone missing – evidence suggests so. nationalists are happy with way it's going – Athens will be pleased etc. PRESS descending.*

It's clear from these notes that I'm not denying myself any creativity. There's barely anything to go on: just the bare bones – the plot points – of a few storylines. The rest is at the back of my mind and in my research notes. With such sketchy notes to hand, the challenge is to produce 500–2,500 words from each set of chapter/section notes. I decide precisely how to do this as I sit to write each day.

Some writers go a step further and plan at a deeper lever, detailing exactly how each plot point will be expanded in a chain of occurrence. They go through each chapter and consider the relative balance of:

- Description
- Dialogue
- Exposition
- Plot points
- Character perspective

- Narrative perspective
- Theme
- Metaphor.

This way, they know in advance what virtually every paragraph will contain. It works for some people, and it might even be a good way to attempt a first novel. I prefer to begin with a blank page and a few structural ideas. But if you do fancy using the approach, it might look like this:

Chapter 4

Plot point(s): Jerry meets Claire in a café and she tells him she's pregnant.

- Omniscient start: describing the café.
- Omniscient: Jerry coming in. Segue into his thoughts via free indirect.
- He orders (choice reflects his character) and sits.
- His thoughts and fears. He observes other people. Sees versions of himself.
- Switch to Claire's perspective as she enters. Sees Jerry as stranger.
- Switch to his perspective seeing her.
- She sits. Awkward chit-chat. Claire comments about feeling sick.
- It comes out and they discuss. Ends badly.
- Perspective of random customer – observing them and deducing situation.

That's a pretty clear guideline for a short chapter, most of which will be dialogue. You can't really go wrong. As I say, this might be handy for a first novel, but practice will see you juggling such decisions automatically as you write.

Narrative approaches in summary

- Match your narrative perspective to the story you want to tell and the characters telling it.

- Ask yourself who is telling the story.
- Should the reader perceive the author at work or be immersed in the thoughts of characters?
- Think about character point of view: who is seeing whom, and how?
- Think about the points you need to cover and what you need to express in each chapter.

Narrative approaches exercises

- Try writing your first paragraph using a few different narrative approaches. Which seems most natural?
- Write a practice scene with one of your characters, experimenting with subject address.
- Create a series of bullets before you write a scene. Does it help you to stay on track?
- Experiment with changing tenses within a paragraph to see what's possible.

6 Case study
Plotting a novel

We've seen most of the elements that go into plotting a novel, but this might not have given you much idea about actually putting it all into practice (especially if you haven't had your idea yet). There's a lot to think about and it can get abstract if you have nothing to apply it to.

In this chapter, I'll look at *The Vice Society* for one last time and go through each of the stages we've discussed – though not necessarily in the order in which we've seen them. How did I turn my original idea into a framework ready for writing?

Start point

After some months of research, I had a collection of scenes, characters, themes and fragmentary storylines I hoped to use. These had been mapped on a spider diagram and I felt I had enough material because there were numerous inter-connections. I also had more scenes than chapters, and enough strong characters for multiple storylines. My cast of major characters was the same as *The Incendiary's Trail*, but I'd also introduced some new ones as villains.

Broad structure

I would follow the pattern of the first book in the series and aim for around thirty chapters of about 3,000 words each. This meant I needed at least thirty major plot points to tell my story: a minimum of one per chapter (but realistically more towards the end).

Table 6.1 Cast of characters for *The Vice Society*

Main characters	Major new characters
George Williamson – ex-detective	'JS' – kingpin pervert
Albert Newsome – detective	James Tattershall – murderer
Sir Richard Mayne – commissioner	Eusebius Bean – spy
Noah Dyson – shrewd chancer	Major Tunnock – pervert
Benjamin – Noah's friend	Mr Poppleton – bookseller
Mr Cullen – ally	

Even before plotting, I knew that I would aim to work with separate, multiple storylines until the mid-point of the novel, after which some catalyst would cause them to meet and spark a gradual increase in pace towards the final climax in the penultimate chapter. A 'rounding-off' chapter would end. This was the broad

Table 6.2 Story-building elements for *The Vice Society*

Storyline ideas	Locations	Themes
– Williamson's wife murdered seven years before. He receives letter	– The Monument – Temple Bar – Scotland Yard – Haymarket	– Temptation of Mr Williamson – Sin and virtue – Revenge
– Newsome keeping a secret ledger of indiscretions and Williamson turns up in it	– Golden Square – Holywell Street – Clerkenwell – Wapping – Smithfield	– Disguise and deception – Covert observation/ spying
– Newsome investigating a fall from a window	– A private asylum – Park Lane residences	– Pornography
– Vice Society taking an unusual interest in Newsome's case	– The British Museum library	
– Noah helps out his friend	– Coffee houses – A brothel	
– Immoral rich men have a debased secret society		

shape of the novel I wanted to write: something like the three three-act structure of a screenplay.

Because I was planning to start with three distinct storylines (requiring the reader to take on a lot of initial detail), I also knew that I needed an engaging first chapter. This would be a prologue set seven years before the main action. I'd come back to it later when Mr Williamson received his pseudonymous letter. Otherwise, the chronology would be conventionally forwards.

Characters

Working with existing characters made it easier, but in fact I'd always conceived my series as a five-book set over which characters would have very long arcs. Those arcs would see the next stage of their development in this novel – something I had worked out before plotting began.

> **Mr Williamson**: his wife long dead, he has dedicated most of his life to the Detective Force until forced out by Inspector Newsome. Increasingly alone and lost, his grief-enforced celibacy is challenged by a foray into the world of pornography and prostitution. Coming into contact with Newsome opens old wounds and increases rivalry.

> **Albert Newsome**: increasingly ambitious, he cares more about catching criminals than observing the law. The case he's assigned by boss Sir Richard Mayne bores him and he's outraged when he's assigned a non-police assistant in the form of Vice Society spy Eusebius Bean. On discovering Mr Williamson is investigating the same case, his suspicions about a high-level conspiracy are fuelled and he risks his career to be first to a solution.

> **Noah Dyson (and friend Benjamin)**: were helped by Mr Williamson in the first book and owe him a favour. They are streetwise and not bound by either Williamson's ethics or Newsome's rules. They can, and will, do anything to help Williamson get revenge on Newsome for what he did to them in the first book.

Eusebius Bean: a maladjusted spy, he is used by powerful men to secretly observe the police investigation into the crime they committed. When he begins to discern the truth, he is in great danger.

Narrative approach

The book is told in retrospect from the point of view of a third-person narrator who is actually part of the story and who reveals himself in first person at critical points. The reasons for this choice were as follows:

- I wanted to use the baroque prose style of the period and thought it would look like an affectation if I did that as an omniscient narrator. It seemed more natural coming from a contemporaneous character.
- By choosing a character from the story as narrator, I could inflect the whole narrative with his personality (he's a cynical and unscrupulous journalist who's following the other characters to make some money). Essentially, I'd be writing in character.
- The series was always going to be about observation and versions of reality. What you saw in the Victorian city wasn't always what it appeared. Thus, his unreliable voice – and his switches from third to first person – shift the reader's perspective at various points, forcing an uneasy ambiguity about what's true.

Storylines

There were three main character storylines (Noah and Benjamin forming part of Williamson's) and these would generally leapfrog each other for the first half of the book. At this stage, the storylines created in the story-building process would have been quite vague: the characters would be pursuing known villains in an investigation that would lead everyone to the same solution. Certain scenes would have been pencilled in. Certain plot points might have been established. Nevertheless, I still had no idea exactly what research material I was going to use, how I was going to fill each chapter, or in which order the storylines would play out. This would be the challenge of the serious plotting.

Plotting

I plot from start to finish on the rationale that the story should grow organically and build on its own foundations. The first thing is to write a chapter number on thirty pages of blank A4 and begin at the first one with the details of what will be in the prologue. With each successive chapter, I ask myself a number of questions to fill the blank page with plot detail:

- Which storyline should come first?
- Which storyline should logically come next?
- How does one chapter play against the previous and the next?
- What plot points should feature?
- How can I make best use of my locations and research detail?
- How is character revealed (in earlier chapters especially) and character arc explored?
- What is happening with pace in each chapter?
- Can I think of any good openers or cliffhangers for each chapter?
- Where is the conflict and/or pressure early in the storylines and how does it play out?
- What can I ask the reader to expect/predict after reading this chapter?
- Am I exploring my themes in an interesting way?

NOTE: At this stage, I STILL DON'T KNOW THE FULL STORY OF THE NOVEL. It's the plotting process that will enable me to move chapter by chapter through it, essentially telling myself the story before I write a word of it. I also have very general diagrams mapping broad movements in terms of pace or storyline. For example, I might have decided that a big set-piece will occur at the mid-point and that another will occur in the penultimate chapter. From my story-building, I already know who the villains are and what motivates them, but I haven't yet plotted the path to these discoveries.

The earlier chapters are the easiest because their role is to *introduce* characters and storylines. They have a clear and necessary role:

Table 6.3 Initial chapters in *The Vice Society*

Chapter	Plot
1	Inspector Newsome – his case. The Vice Society. Refer to Williamson: ex-colleague.
2	Mr Williamson – his new job working on postal fraud.
3	Newsome working his case with Mr Cullen. Someone is spying on them.
4	Eusebius Bean – his mission and his shady boss.

Thus, in the first four chapters, I have introduced my main characters, their world, their concerns and their storylines. I have additionally included some interesting research detail for the reader's pleasure (details of postal fraud in Victorian England, the historically genuine Vice Society, police procedure and the fabric of 1840s London).

As result of this beginning, I may also know, for example, that Williamson will now be appearing in Chapters 5, 7, 11 and 15, etc. This is because his storyline is woven between others in the first half the book. Similarly, I might know that Newsome will feature in Chapters 6, 8 or 10. This is mere structural necessity – once a storyline has begun, I'll keep going back to it and moving between different ones.

Nevertheless, I STILL DON'T KNOW THE FULL STORY OF THE NOVEL. I don't know why the man fell out of the window in Holywell Street. I don't know exactly how the Vice Society is involved (only that it is somehow) and I don't know exactly when Mr Williamson is going to get the letter about his wife's murder. This is what's going to be in the next chapters. At this stage, I'm building story and its framework simultaneously.

As I work forward from my foundation chapters and look ahead to the interwoven chapter/storyline structure, I ask myself further questions:

- What clues or plot points in previous chapters can link to the next chapters in that storyline sequence? Each chapter should prefigure the next (and reference the last) in its own storyline. How are the character arcs progressing? What plot points have I seeded? Am I monitoring pace?
- What *could* happen in the next chapter? A discovery? A revelation? Another death? What would be the most exciting/logical next step, bearing in mind my existing story fragments?
- How far away is my next plot point and what's the best way to get there? Am I including enough texture to keep my reader interested?

This can be a slow and sometimes frustrating process: basically making up a very long and complicated story step by step while also considering all of those factors mentioned in the chapter on Construction. In the case of *The Vice Society*, I think it took a month of daily noodling before I had a workable plot – plot in terms of a 30-piece progression of story including character arcs and thematic explorations. I'd think about it while cycling to work, while at work, while eating. It would come to me a plot point at a time: Williamson should visit his wife's grave for pathos, Newsome should read about Williamson in his secret ledger, the villain should try to entrap one of the detectives.

Inevitably, I'd get stuck sometimes and wind up in a storyline cul-de-sac. I might get to Chapter 17 and realise nothing else could happen. How could I move from where I was to where I needed to be – to the next logical plot point? Such situations require pause and reassessment. It's often necessary to go back over what you've plotted so far and look for gaps or patterns. Adding something earlier (a clue, a comment) might create a new possibility in the place where you're stuck. For example, I decided quite late in the plotting process of this book that the villain would be given away by his unusual perfume. This meant I had to go back and leave traces of it in earlier chapters.

It's also very handy to draw on the work from the story-building stage. There might be material in your research notes that can help you out of the tight plotting spot. Perhaps it's a location, or a facet of theme, or some interesting detail you can work into the storyline. For example, I had no idea how I was going to use Temple Bar in my story – only that it seemed a fascinating location. When the time came to decide how and where Williamson would meet Noah for a secret rendezvous, the choice seemed obvious.

At other times, introducing an incidental character will offer a solution. In the chapter where Williamson and Benjamin go to Clerkenwell to seek clues about a man thrown in the Fleet river there, I needed a way for some clues to become evident. An eye-witness seemed the easiest way, so I created the butcher's son Roger: a grimy urchin who (I suddenly decided) was actually in the employ of the villains.

I occasionally surprise myself. At one stage, I was plotting a chapter where Noah Dyson goes to a bookshop to question its owner. The plot point involved the shop owner being very evasive and thus showing he was guilty. By this stage, I was drawing close to the mid-point of the book where I wanted all the storylines to meet, but I still had little idea how this might be effected. I was also conscious that I needed to add a bit of pace to pick up the novel after a lot of exposition. And suddenly it came to me: I would have Inspector Newsome raid the bookshop as part of his own investigation and find Noah there with Mr Williamson. It would be a great cliffhanger and the next chapter would be the key central point of the novel.

The benefit of having the plot all laid out before you write means that when you get to Chapter 17 and realise that something can't happen here because you hadn't laid the groundwork before, you simply jot a note in Chapters 2 and 7 so the plot point in Chapter 17 suddenly *does* become possible. No fuss! Alternatively, you might decide to switch the order of some chapters or plot points to manage pace or storyline interplay. Either way, it's as easy as changing a number. You can see from an aerial, objective, view what the broad sweep of your plot looks like and where it might be too thick or thin.

My chapter notes tend to be very sketchy – probably not the sort of thing that anyone else could pick up and write from. By this stage, I've done so much research and story-building that I pretty much know what I'm going to write and the plot provides prompts for me so I don't get lost. For example, the original, pencilled, plot notes for Chapter 15 of *The Vice Society* read:

> *Newsome. Feelings about Bean? Waterman murdered on H street. Circumstances? Found by who? Seen by Bean talking to W'son. Newsome finds out W was with prostitute. Realises he's on same case. Waterman was tortured and washed out of Fleet river (heavy rain). Must have been tortured at Clerkenwell (only part of city open to river due to building work – excuse to go there)*

There are a number of plot points here. The rest – locations, dialogue, description, etc. – will be filled in a few months down the line when I get to Chapter 15. By then, I'll have fourteen other written chapters under my belt and certain things may have changed. In fact, the actual, published Chapter 15 of *Vice Society* does not feature any of this information. It's about Noah. Somewhere along the line, I must have added a chapter or changed the order.

The process simply continues chapter by chapter until the end and/or until I have sufficient detail to begin writing. Or rather, I tend to leave the climactic scene largely unplotted. I know where it's going to take place, who will be in it and what needs to happen, but it's so far down the line that the plot may have changed by up to 30 per cent by then. Better to write it when I get there.

The final plot for *The Vice Society* was thirty loose pages of pencilled notes, although you could have fitted them on eight A4 pages if the spaces were removed. They comprised:

- Plot points for each chapter
- Character detail per chapter as required
- The final order of the storylines
- Notes on openers or cliffhangers as required
- Notes to myself to cross-reference certain points between chapters.

To summarise, I had created the storylines of the book before I had written a word, arranging and rearranging a multitude of scenes, arcs, storylines, episodes and locations so that I could see clear narrative lines throughout the whole. Any weaknesses or gaps were visible well in advance. Most importantly, I had confidence in the book I was about to write – I knew it would work and knew *how* it would work. No matter how difficult the actual writing might be, I'd have the comfort of knowing where I was going with it: forwards, always forwards.

You may decide to take a slightly different approach. Every writer creates their own process. The important thing is that you understand *in advance of the writing process* what mechanisms will make your book readable and therefore more publishable. You won't write a chapter or a scene without knowing – somewhere at the back of your writer's mind – how that scene contributes to the much larger fabric of the novel. Perhaps it adds pace or character detail, builds tone or furthers the story. Perhaps it's a thematic riff or groundwork for a later twist. The point is: if it has no narrative function, it's redundant. You'll probably cut it later.

The plot document

This was not, however, the document I used to write the novel. A few loose pages could easily be lost. Plus, they didn't contain any of my research material (which was scribbled in notebooks). Now it was time to open a digital document.

I transferred the plot notes (making occasional last-minute refinements) into a document as numbered chapters. Then I went through my research notebooks and added all the relevant detail to those chapters that required it. For example, the chapter set at Temple Bar featured the plot points and all my notes about that location: the sights, the smells and the impressions from a dozen primary sources (including a visit to the place itself). This was all I needed to write each chapter.

The final plot document was about twenty typed A4 pages of plot points and research notes – a totally self-contained resource that I could take with me anywhere. No need to refer back to the original notebooks or check a fact. No fear of losing a page. With this document, I could write at work, on a train, at home or in a hotel and always have my materials to hand. At any stage, I could skip forward and check a plot detail so I could write consistently towards it in a suspenseful way. If I'd wanted to, I could have written the book in any order because I knew all the pieces.

Perhaps most importantly, having the entire plot laid out like this meant that if I drifted from it as I wrote – or if I had better ideas along the way – I could amend forthcoming chapter notes so that the changes could be absorbed without fuss. Far from being a controlling force, the plot document becomes obsolete with each completed chapter. The final version of the plot is the finished novel itself.

NOTE: The plot document – in whatever form you choose to write it – is a form of literary security. It's your promise to yourself that you won't get lost or blocked. No matter how busy your life, you can open the plot document, look at what you've written so far, look at the notes for the next bit and start writing in the sure knowledge that you're not wasting time or words. This is a professional process.

As mentioned earlier, some writers may want to drift and float within their first draft, following their mood and seeing where the writing takes them. This can be fun, but it almost never results in a competent first draft. It will need re-working and re-working. It's one way of learning how to write a novel. At some stage, this method has to acknowledge all of the same structural requirements of the more ordered process. For me, that's like finishing a meal and remembering you forgot to season it – so you eat a spoon of pepper.

Case study in summary

- Gather your materials from the story-building stage: characters, episodes, themes, potential story-threads.
- Consider the broad structural requirements of the novel: beginning–middle–end, introductions, dénouements.
- Look at character and plot. Which is driving the storyline(s)?
- Think about character arcs.
- Begin ordering and plotting storylines while . . .
- Keep in mind structural elements (pace, cliffhangers, storyline juxtaposition, etc.).
- Be methodical and develop techniques for moving the story forward.
- Create a finished plot document to work from.

7 Troubleshooting

At the beginning of the book, we looked at some common structural problems in first novels. Having gone through various stages of pre-writing preparation, let's look at them again and ask why they might have occurred.

Table 7.1 Troubleshooting

Problem	Probable cause
Unclear narrative point of view	The writer hadn't decided beforehand on the best way to present the story and characters. Perhaps the story has come together in pieces over a prolonged period and through numerous drafts so that there's no narrative consistency.
Summarising rather than narrating	A classic sign of beginning writing with just a loose idea of story but no plot structure and little character work. The only way the author can tell the story is to summarise it, because he hasn't got enough texture, plot points or occurrence to allow the story to reveal itself. The writer may also not have grasped showing and telling; he is writing as a reader. More work at the story-building stage would have helped.

(continued)

Table 7.1 (continued)

Problem	Probable cause
Halting structure	The writer has a number of scenes in mind, but has probably done insufficient planning in combining them into a coherent plot with interconnections, consistent pace and texture. He is writing as a reader, hoping it will all gel on its own. There has to be an overarching plot.
The premise is weak	Simply, the idea hasn't been built and expanded into a plot by a story-building stage. What seemed like a good idea is gradually diluted with the ever-increasing word count and a lack of developmental plot points. It's writing as a reader again, hoping the book will go somewhere on its own.
Diffuse and disconnected storylines	The writer was unable to choose between different ideas and decided to use all of them (perhaps in an attempt to make word count). Or, the initial idea was to use multiple storylines but insufficient plotting was done to make them work together. Or, the writer started with a few storylines and became more interested in one at the expense of the others (writing as a reader).
Not enough occurrence	Simply, a lack of plotting. The writer has ideas, characters and some story, but he has not achieved an aerial view of the novel – and therefore of the story – through plotting and has lost track of what's happening story-wise at a chapter level (ultimately, not very much).
Occurrence unevenly distributed	The writer has a strong idea about parts of his storyline, but has not made the story unfold consistently. If there is a plot, there are too few plot points, too widely spaced.
Rushed or inconclusive ending	Simply, the writer didn't know what to write because he didn't have a sufficient grasp on the factors that had built the story until this point. A climax should grow organically from its narrative foundations, not be dropped in. A good plot would have shown what kind of ending was appropriate.

It's clear that all of these problems could have been avoided by being prepared to write the novel: prepared in terms of ability and in terms of thinking it through. Novels with these kinds of issues tend to go through many drafts. Many are never finished. Fewer still are published. They cause their writers years of frustration and engender the erroneous sense that writing a novel is almost impossible.

It is hard work, but it's also possible to write a novel without this sort of frustration. A few weeks' planning can eradicate most of the problems you'll face once you begin writing. And let's be clear; it's the writing that's the really hard work if you're doing it properly. One acquaintance has described writing a novel as going into a very long tunnel at high speed. Once you're in there, you don't want to stop. You want to get to the light at the end as quickly and as safely as possible. That's what the next part is about.

Troubleshooting in summary

Preliminary work eradicates most of the problems of writing a novel!

8   Before you write a word

So you've got a workable plot and you're ready to start your novel. You couldn't be in a better position. But there are a few more things to consider before you sit down at the keyboard or the notebook.

Scheduling

It's estimated that the average novel takes about two years. Some take days; others take decades. This is not to say you should begin your novel with no idea of how long it's going to take. If it gets published, you'll be expected to produce a second book pretty quickly and therefore it's good practice to establish certain productive behaviours in advance. This is the professional approach.

You should already have a good idea – from your years of practice – how much you can realistically produce in a day or an hour. Set yourself a daily goal: 500 words, two hours of writing – whatever works. It's important to be realistic. If all you can manage is 300 words a day (Graham Greene's daily output), then do 300. That way, you'll be able to set a deadline for when you'll reach your 90,000 words.

You have to stick to your plans. There's nothing worse than seeing your novel slip away from you as other things get in the way. Besides, it's really a fallacy that you have to sit at your computer all day, every day, for years to complete a novel. I've never done more than three hours a day – usually two – and these can be fitted quite easily even into a full working day. With practice, your hourly word count will increase and you'll be able to knock out 1,000–2,000 words in a couple of hours depending on your typing speed. This, of course, depends on your having a plot to work to. If you have no idea where you're going, you'll have to spend some of your precious daily time thinking or worrying or being 'blocked'.

How strict should you be with yourself? That depends on how serious you are about your book. I take a laptop on holiday with me during a novel. Only very severe illness will stop me (I've done my daily word count with a broken elbow and a torn shoulder-tendon on different occasions). It's not about obsessiveness, it's about the sheer pleasure of writing. And obsessiveness.

There is also comfort in the basic mathematics of writing. One thousand words a day for ninety days is a novel. A novel in three months. This is entirely possible when you have a comprehensive plot to work from. In 2012, I wrote 250,000 words while doing three part-time jobs. In 2015, I wrote two 80,000-word novels in eight months (the novels themselves took eighteen weeks in total).

> *Two hours of writing fiction leaves this writer completely drained. For those two hours he has been in a different place with totally different people.*
> Roald Dahl (cited in Price, 2013)

Document security

There's nothing worse than losing your novel. Even 1,000 words of excellent writing accidentally deleted can be a trauma. I thought I'd lost my third novel entirely when a bug in my laptop filled the document with 100 pages of weird code. Fortunately, I was able to reconstruct the finished document from previous, stored versions. It pays to be safe. Some strategies you might employ include:

- Saving your document every few paragraphs, or setting your computer to do this automatically.
- Saving your document to a memory stick after each writing session.

- Emailing yourself (or a trusted friend) a copy of the document every few days.
- Changing the document name and resaving if you're using different machines.
- Saving the document in different formats (e.g. PDF) just in case.
- Keeping all previous versions in case you need to go back and reconstruct.
- Printing sections and keeping them in case a nuclear explosion creates an electromagnetic pulse that wipes out all electronic devices.
- Keeping a version on a memory stick at work or with a friend in case your house burns down.

Some of these may seem a little paranoid, but you end up feeling quite maternal about your novel when you've spent months writing 100,000 words. The most I've ever actually lost is a large paragraph, and I still resent the fact.

What to expect

Of course it'll be difficult. There will be days when you'd rather gnaw off a limb than do your word count. It's not that you hate the writing (Mr Vonnegut), it's that you love the writing so much that you feel the terrible weight of self-expectation. But there can be no excuses. There can be no 'in the mood'. You have a plot; you know what's coming next; you are a writer. So you write. This is the difference between aspiring writers and writers. Only when you truly accept you have no other option but to sit and do it will you give in.

It's OK when you begin to drift from the plot that you've gone to so much trouble to create. This is inevitable. It's even desirable. Characters develop. You have brilliant ideas. Suddenly, the story is coming alive in ways you could never have predicted. But it's doing this largely because you had a good framework to work to. And it's the framework that will allow you to follow your ideas without losing track of the novel. Work your new ideas into the structure and keep it all focused. If necessary, plot a new spider diagram from the new point you've reached. Remind yourself: there's no such thing as block – just lack of practice or planning.

There will be days when you're convinced it's all rubbish, that you're wasting your time. Fear will grip you. Perhaps someone reads a section of your manuscript and doesn't make the right faces. No matter. Look again at your plot and see all the great scenes you're going to write. Remind yourself of this great character or that great scene you wrote the previous week. The worst that can happen is that this book will make you an even better writer. The best that can happen is that all the gainsayers will abase themselves at your feet when you win the Nobel.

Above all, resist the temptation to go back and start reading stuff you wrote weeks ago. If you don't like it, your confidence will be critically injured. You have your plot. Follow it to the end and finish the book. However good or bad it is, it will be *finished*. Editing will cure it of whatever illnesses it may have picked up along the way, but an unfinished novel is no use to anyone.

And when you've finished, don't fetishise this novel you've produced. You're a better writer at the end of it than you were when you started. Your next book will be better still. Being a novelist isn't about producing one novel. Nor is it about ever really being satisfied. The pleasure is surely in the ever-diminishing possibility of one day writing the 'perfect novel'. *Somebody* has to. Why not you?

Good luck.

Writing a book is a horrible, exhausting struggle, like a long bout of some painful illness. One would never undertake such a thing if one were not driven on by some demon whom one can neither resist nor understand.

George Orwell (2004)

You fail only if you stop writing.

Ray Bradbury (cited in Strickland, 1992)

Thematic reading list

There are numerous guides on how to write a novel, but the very best way to learn how to perfect your writing is to study and dissect good novels with a writerly eye. Having read this book, you're now in a better position to look at some of the following titles for more lessons. There will be much thematic crossover here, as you'll see if you read all of them.

Episodic novels

On Her Majesty's Secret Service, Ian Fleming
The Odyssey, Homer
Don Quixote, Cervantes
The Innocents Abroad, Mark Twain (a travelogue more than a novel)
Moby Dick, Herman Melville.

Pure commercial fiction

The Da Vinci Code, Dan Brown (biggest seller in UK publishing history)
The Girl with the Dragon Tattoo, Stieg Larsson
Kane and Abel, Jeffrey Archer
Valley of the Dolls, Jacqueline Susann
Gone with the Wind, Margaret Mitchell
The Godfather, Mario Puzo
Eye of the Needle, Ken Follett
Live and Let Die, Ian Fleming.

Conspiracy novels

Libra, Don de Lillio
Foucault's Pendulum, Umberto Eco
Bleeding Edge, Thomas Pynchon
The Underworld Trilogy, James Ellroy.

Novels with unusual chronologies

Time's Arrow, Martin Amis
Slaughterhouse 5, Kurt Vonnegut
Hawksmoor, Peter Ackroyd
The Master and Margarita, Mikhail Bulgakov
The Good Soldier, Ford Madox Ford.

'Plotless' novels

Suttree, Cormac McCarthy
Tropic of Cancer, Henry Miller
Tristram Shandy, Laurence Sterne
Death on Credit, Louis-Ferdinand Céline
Molloy, Malone Dies, The Unnamable (trilogy), Samuel Beckett.

Allegorical novels

Lord of the Flies, William Golding
Gulliver's Travels, Jonathan Swift
Fahrenheit 451, Ray Bradbury
A Clockwork Orange, Anthony Burgess
Animal Farm, George Orwell.

Unreliable narration novels

Pale Fire, Vladimir Nabokov
Remains of the Day, Kazuo Ishiguro
Fight Club, Chuck Palahniuk
Catcher in the Rye, J.D. Salinger.

Novels with interesting narrative approaches

Madame Bovary, Gustave Flaubert
Bonfire of the Vanities, Tom Wolfe
King, Queen, Knave, Vladimir Nabokov
Timequake, Kurt Vonnegut
Journey to the End of the Night, Louis-Ferdinand Céline
Bright Lights, Big City, Jay McInerney
USA (trilogy), John Dos Passos
Ulysses, James Joyce
Mrs Dalloway, Virginia Woolf.

'Voice' novels

Money, Martin Amis
Lolita, Vladimir Nabokov
Earthly Powers, Anthony Burgess.

Highly descriptive 'place' novels

The Shipping News, E. Annie Proulx
Blood Meridian, Cormac McCarthy
Oliver Twist, Charles Dickens
In Search of Lost Time, Marcel Proust
Heart of Darkness, Joseph Conrad.

Novels with deceptively simple writing

Factotum, Charles Bukowski
The Old Man and the Sea, Ernest Hemingway
Road Dogs, Elmore Leonard
The Maltese Falcon, Dashiell Hammett
Gold, Blaise Cendrars.

Wild-card oddities

To the End of the World, Blaise Cendrars
Inherent Vice, Thomas Pynchon
The Erasers, Alain Robbe-Grillet
Catch-22, Joseph Heller
Any stories by Edgar Allan Poe.

References

Baker, Carlos (1992). *Hemingway: The Writer as Artist*, Princeton University Press

Bradbury, Ray (2015). *Zen in the Art of Writing*, HarperCollins

Burgess, Anthony (1990). *You've Had Your Time*, William Heinemann

Camfield, Gregg (2003). *The Oxford Companion to Mark Twain*, Oxford University Press

Carter, Angela (2012). *Expletives Deleted: Selected Writings*, Random House

Earnshaw, Steven (2014). *The Handbook of Creative Writing*, Edinburgh University Press

Felstead, Sherree A (2014). *Passion to Paper: A Simple Recipe for Writing your Personal Story,* Balboa Press

Gabriel, Susan (2014). *Fearless Writing for Women: Extreme Encouragement and Writing Inspirations,* Susan Gabriel

Goldman, William (2010). *Adventures in the Screen Trade,* Hachette UK

Graham, David (2014). *The Philosophy of Mark Twain: The Wit and Wisdom of a Literary Genius,* David Graham

King, Stephen (2012). *On Writing,* Hodder Paperbacks

Mailer, Norman (2003). *The Spooky Art: Thoughts on Writing*, Random House

McLuhan, Marshall and Lapham, Lewis (2003). *Understanding Media: The Extensions of Man*, McGraw-Hill

Oates, Joyce Carol and Milazzo, Lee (ed.) (1989). *Conversations with Joyce Carol Oates*, University Press of Mississippi

Orwell, George (2004). *Why I Write,* Penguin

Osborn, Susan Titus (2001). *A Complete Guide to Writing for Publication*, ACW Press

Price, Stephen D. (2013). *The Little Book of Writers' Wisdom,* Skyhorse Publishing Inc

Priest, Stephen (ed.) (2002). *Jean-Paul Sartre: Basic Writings*, Routledge
Sedaris, David (n.d.) Attributed
Somerset Maugham, W. (2014) *Orientations*, A Word to the Wise
Strickland, Bill (1992). *On Being a Writer*, F&W Media Inc
Vonnegut, Kurt (2010). *Palm Sunday,* Random House
Weis, Daniel (2010). *Everlasting Wisdom,* Paragon Publishing
The Guardian (2014), 4 March
The Guardian (2009), 20 June
Times Literary Supplement (2010), 3 September

Index